THE

COMMONWEALTH

OF LIFE

THE

COMMONWEALTH

OF LIFE

A Treatise on Stewardship Economics

Peter G. Brown

Montréal/New York/London

Black Rose Books No. EE299

Hardcover ISBN: 1-55164-199-2 (bound) Paperback ISBN: 1-55164-198-4 (pbk.)

Canadian Cataloguing in Publication Data

Brown, Peter G.

The commonwealth of life : a treatise on stewardship economics

Includes bibliographical references and index.
Hardcover ISBN: 1-55164-199-2 (bound) Paperback ISBN: 1-55164-198-4 (pbk.)

1. Economics—Moral and ethical aspects. 2. Political ethics. 3. Environmental ethics.
4. Human rights. 5. International relations—Moral and ethical aspects. I. Title.

BJ1031.B76 2001   172   C2001-901163-6

Cover design by Associés libres, Montréal

C.P. 1258	2250 Military Road	99 Wallis Road
Succ. Place du Parc	Tonawanda, NY	London, E9 5LN
Montréal, H2W 2R3	14150	England
Canada	USA	UK

To order books in North America:
(phone) 1-800-565-9523 (fax) 1-800-221-9985
In Europe: (phone) London 44 (0)20 8986-4854 (fax) 44 (0)20 8533-5821

Our Web Site address: http://www.web.net/blackrosebooks

A publication of the Institute of Policy Alternatives of Montréal (IPAM)

Printed in Canada

The Canada Council | Le Conseil des Arts
for the Arts | du Canada

CONTENTS

Part II Fiduciary Institutions

Part III   Transparent Sovereignty

FOREWORD

Peter Brown's book *The Commonwealth of Life* defends a certain version of cosmopolitanism or global ethics and contrasts it to other ethical approaches including rival forms of global ethics. By a global ethic, or what I called in my own book a 'world ethic,' is meant an ethical theory which asserts both certain universal values, i.e., values to be accepted anywhere, and also responsibilities or duties which are global in scale.

In defending his own view Brown is particularly critical of the growth model of mainstream economics, and linked to this both the libertarian ethic lying behind it and the 'morality of states' approach to international relations. In their place he develops a theory of stewardship economics which takes proper account of the 'commonwealth of life', and a theory of trusteeship and transparent sovereignty in which the role of governments is to protect the basic rights of all, including those falling outside their respective political communities. At the core of this approach is a commitment to three basic rights, adapted from Locke: the rights to bodily integrity, to religious, moral and political choice, and to subsistence. Indeed the whole account is presented as essentially a *Lockean* account.

The style is robust, the theses controversial and challenging. Readers may find themselves surprised that Locke is used to defend an essentially biocentric, green economics and global perspective. Was not Locke, as a person of his times, essentially anthropocentric, a defender of capitalist property and presenter of a bounded 'citizen' account of obligation within a political community via the social contract? We can of course to some extent pick and choose what we take to be the 'core' elements of historical figures, and there is, to say the least, something refreshing about Brown's use of Locke in these ways. There are times when he seems quicker to contrast his views than he might with alternative views, especially if one distinguishes between what some might do or advocate in the name of an idea and the idea itself. For instance, sustainability and humanitarianism are both contrasted, though it seems that both these ideas are sufficiently flexible that they could be interpreted to incorporate the ideas which Brown himself wants to advocate.

No one who reads this book will fail to notice the energy and passion which runs through the text. Here is a man who cares about the world we live in and, in the words of the early Quaker William Penn, 'endeavours to mend it'. At the same time there is evidence of much learning in relation to the issues which have engaged those in the philosophy and public affairs arena. In this respect he clearly fulfils the aim—one which is sure to be controversial for some—of combining academic integrity with an agenda for radical change.

Nigel Dower, author of *World Ethics: The New Agenda*,
and editor of the Edinburgh Studies in World Ethics series

PREFACE

I recently moved to Canada, a country where the idea of the commonwealth still resonates. I found here a place where Locke's natural rights are important, and where his conception of natural law responsibilities goes hand in hand with those rights. It is a place with a tempered ambivalence toward the idea of unlimited growth, a country with a relatively small human population, and vast prairies, mountains, tundra, rivers, and oil and gas deposits. Despite these generous moral and physical endowments, the future of Canada is insecure within and it charts an uncertain and wavering course in the world at large. Its values, history, and geography give it compass, but it often seems to have lost sight of the chart.

The Canadian right wing press claim that too much government control has caused Canadians to enjoy a lower standard of living than in the United States: that after-tax incomes are lower and that productivity lags. There is something to this concern with over-governance. However, there are costs associated with economic growth, and the analytical framework employed by these advocates has no way of accounting for these. In addition—and this is a symmetrical mistake—critics of over-governance proceed as if all taxes are only costs instead of seeing them as costs which pay for benefits, for example, what we pay for health care or environmental protection. Canada also wavers about its role in the international economic order. It rhetorically embraces the goal of reducing greenhouse gases while encouraging energy exports to our profligate neighbor to the south. It flirts with the idea of bulk exports of water, despite the fact that the faucet would be hard to turn off once turned on. Canada's fascination with the neo-classical abyss is dangerous.

Canada needs to engage in a critical appraisal of its future in the context of the commonwealth of life: the interlocking web of life to which we owe respect. In this book I stress the need to re-conceptualize economics, governance, and civil society in order to have a just and enduring international order. The situation is dire. Ecological destruction is growing, and becoming more widespread under the twin attacks of careening economic growth and the rapid increase in human population. And the growth ethic has spread under the wings of globalization: the destruction it brings has at once become greater and its effects often less visible to the more affluent countries. Though the rate of population growth has slowed in many areas (and even reversed in some) the absolute numbers of persons continues to grow at an overall rate that is sure to transform the commonwealth of life, however resilient, in tragically foreseeable ways.

Our problems are profound and widespread. We use new compounds to create innovative products, which in turn stimulate economic growth by making the old versions obsolete. As more and more growth is stimulated around the world, the pace of change quickens. We, and our decedents, are becoming "Red Queens," running ever faster just to stay in place, as if in Alice's *Wonderland*. Through chemical engineering we have created thousands of compounds that are not found in nature. The commonwealth of life has not made evolutionary adaptation to their effects, and now it is also dawning on us that we need to worry not just about these compounds individually, but also about their effects when one or more of them interact, or when they interact with myriad life forms on our planet.

We have created a combinatorial explosion.

To solve these problems we must rethink the makeup of industrial society as a whole. We in the industrial world have created a complex of management problems that cannot be solved by incremental steps along the same ill-chosen path. We need to reflect on how we got to this dangerous place.

The institutions of higher education bear considerable responsibility. As the tough-minded social critic David Orr has pointed out, we have failed to ask: What is education for? We have assumed that more knowledge is always better, but this is not necessarily true: in developing new chemical compounds we have linearly increased our knowledge but we have exponentially increased our ignorance. We must remember and learn, or perhaps *re*-learn, that we are embedded in the natural world.

The study of thermodynamics and ecology is essential in any education worthy of the name. We must look for the consequences of what we know and learn. We need ethical frameworks that lead us to question and examine the results of our teaching and research on the natural and human communities of which we are a part. We should be well past the stage where we favor innovation for its own sake. Of any issue we should ask: What is this good for? And recognize too that our education must be not only *of* the world but *in* it. Most of my students come from urban or suburban settings. When I discuss Thoreau's *Walden* with them, I am struck by the fact that many do not know what a woodchuck is, many do not know if they have ever seen the morning star.

Education must be seen as an element in the covenant we have with the commonwealth of life. Technology must have a justified purpose. There is a way to reduce and perhaps—over the course of several decades —substantially mitigate the "Red Queen" effect by re-conceptualizing scientific and technological development so that it is not at cross-purposes with natural systems.

The task before us is monumental: to re-envision our place in the world, from lords and masters to citizens and stewards. Nevertheless, the building blocks are within our reach. Our fore-bearers have given us the tools to refashion our future: the rule of law, science, the market, private property, a free press, the protection of the weak. These and a myriad of other hallmarks of our progress and vision as a species are essential elements in a refashioned future in the commonwealth of life. With courage and resolve we can re-ground education, reinvent industrial society, re-design economics, rediscover trustee government, and redirect civil society in service to the commonwealth of life.

A new relationship with life and the world is within our grasp. The inaugural golden age is still before us, ours to make, but we had better hurry. Time is of the essence.

Montreal
July 2001

To all creatures great and small

ACKNOWLEDGMENTS

A variety of works by others have substantially influenced this volume. Nigel Dower's *World Ethics: The New Agenda* helped to frame my thinking about the need for a cosmopolitan ethic. Henry Shue's *Basic Rights* shaped much of my thinking about the nature of rights and the transboundary obligations that go with them that is set out in Chapter 1. James Rachels' *Created from Animals: The Moral Implications of Darwinism* and Farley Mowat's *Sea of Slaughter* heavily influenced the argument in Chapter 2. Karl Polanyi's *The Great Transformation*, Robert Skidelsky's books on the life and work of Keynes and numerous writings of and conversations with my colleague at the University of Maryland, Herman Daly, and Neva Goodwin of Tufts University, helped me see – as put forward in Chapter 3 – that an entirely new framework for macroeconomics was needed. Richard Ashcraft's *Revolutionary Politics and Locke's Two Treatises of Government* helped me to see the relationship between Locke's theory of natural rights and his theory of natural law which lies beneath the description of trustee government set out in Chapter 4. Elinor Ostrom's *Governing the Commons: The Evolution of Institutions for Collective Action* (and again Polany's *The Great Transformation*) helped me to see the way out of the dilemma of public versus private responses to environmental problems that forms much of the argument in Chapter 5. Lastly, Charles Beitz' *Political Theory and International Relations* revealed the confused nature of the discourse about the relations between nations, and hence gave shape to Chapter 6.

I am grateful to numerous people who thoughtfully reviewed this manuscript. These include Peter Balint, Worth Bateman, Fred Branfman, David Seaton Brown, Donald Brown, John Buell, Herman Daly, Anne Edwards, Jaye Ellis, Nancy Fessenden, Myron Frankman, Neva Goodwin, Margaret Graham, Michael Howard, David Korten, Mary Midgley, Ossama Mikhail, Robert Nelson, Seema Paul, Thomas Schelling, Michael Shuman, John Van Tine, and Mick Womersley. Robert Hunt Sprinkle and Ethan Walden Brown provided brilliant, patient, and constructive criticism for numerous chapters. Nigel Dower had the vision to see that a world ethic is required. He provided patient and trenchant criticisms of numerous drafts of it. Steve Fetter supplied the table in the appendix, and Marcia Waterway helped me find the diagram on page 50. Paget Graham provided invaluable assistance in preparing the final typescript, Ann Vinnicombe carefully edited it, and Christian Abizaid proofed the galleys.

My thinking on this subject has benefitted from discussion and correspondence with Grace Bateman, Holly Dressel, Daniel Levitin, John Lipman, Steve Maguire, Suzy Moore, Thomas Naylor and Joseph Rasmussen. My thanks also to Linda Barton and Dimitri Roussopoulos of Black Rose Books for their encouragement. Defects are my own.

INTRODUCTION

I write to chart a new direction for the human future, and the future of the rest of life with which we share this planet. To do this I propose a new global ethic. This new direction requires bringing philosophical order to the conceptually incoherent relations between and among nations. This, in turn, requires a rethinking and regrounding of the institutions of markets, government, and civil society. And this cannot be done without establishing a firm foundation on which to rest advancing the human estate and protecting and reconstructing the commonwealth of life: the biosphere of which we are a citizen. Hence, I begin by developing this foundation in Part One; trace the implications of it for institutions in Part Two; and then set forth the implications of the foundation and these institutions for the relations among nations in Part Three.

The actions of national governments, markets, the institutions of civil society, and individual persons should be open to scrutiny. That is, they should be *transparent* to examination and subject to sanctions for violating international norms designed to protect, enhance and restore human rights; and to protect, enhance and restore the commonwealth of life. I will argue in favor of what I call a *fiduciary or trustee* perspective: that public policy and private conduct alike be framed within a set of duties to care for each other and the rest of the biosphere in perpetuity.

My motivations are largely practical. As I write, there is vast, unnecessary human suffering in our world and needless waste of ecological and other natural resources. The killing rampage that has characterized the twentieth century continues in widespread wars with escalating civilian casualties and tens of millions of refugees. The number of persons who are malnourished, who live in regions with severe air pollution, who lack safe drinking water, inexpensive vaccinations, and reliable birth control is in the hundreds of millions. The human population grows by hundreds of millions per decade. Nuclear, biological, and conventional weapons proliferate, while control over existing stockpiles declines in the former Soviet Bloc.

1

The loss of biodiversity accelerates. Huge amounts of topsoil are eroded. Streams and estuaries are clogged degrading, even eradicating, once abundant life. World fisheries decline, even collapse. Coral reefs are dying. Carbon-dioxide emissions soar, further destabilizing world climate. Deforestation is widespread. Prime farmland is paved. Vast fires rage seasonally in many of the world's tropical forests. Polar ecosystems are fragmenting.

These are certain signs of policy failure and moral bewilderment. The first step is to see how we have led ourselves astray. As Barbara Tuchman has so aptly noted: 'We live in an age of collapsing assumptions.'[1] We have falsely assumed that: the human well-being can be measured by economic growth; that humans enjoy a unique moral place in the universe; we can safely predict the consequences of our actions; that nation states are morally privileged; that markets and democracy are mutually reinforcing institutions; and that the world is largely unperturbed and unperturbable by human actions. We have thus three challenges ahead of us. First, to come up with an adequate account of our minimal obligations to each other, and to the rest of the natural order. Second, to redefine and reshape the institutions of economics, government, and civil society to reflect these obligations. Third, and last, to reconceptualize and redirect the relations between nations so as to foster these institutions and discharge these obligations.

To do this we must: (1) Provide an account of human welfare. (2) Respond to the human propensity to violence. (3) Have an account of the duties of citizens and local, national, and global institutions. (4) Respect non-human organisms and ecological systems. (5) Accommodate complex adaptive systems: systems that have multiple feedback loops not reducible to their parts. (6) Reflect the fact that the nation state itself is in a period of rapid transformation, accompanied by significant decline in its traditional powers. (7) Address the fact that neither markets nor demo-cracy are self-maintaining institutions, but that each requires constant discipline and nourishment. (8) Explicitly admit that human beings significantly effect global geophysical systems.

Getting from where we are to transparent sovereignty in the common-wealth of life will be a long road. We seek to overturn and/or redirect powerful interests. Hence setting our foot along that road will take courage. We must not be content with marginal adjustments. We must hold ourselves and our institutions to unfamiliar, but not unknown, fiduciary standards. Time is of the essence. We must move with all deliberate speed. I seek not so much to convince those who do not weep at the tragedies we have brought upon ourselves and the rest of life with whom we share this planet. Rather my goal is to make manifest to those who are saddened that there is an alternative way of thinking about the future. There are those who can live with the status quo, and those who cannot. This book is written for those who cannot.

Montreal
August 1999

NOTES

1. Barbara W. Tuchman, *A Distant Mirror: The Calamitous 14th Century*, p. xxx.

PART I
PROGRESS
AND THE
COMMONWEALTH
OF LIFE

INTRODUCTION

Part One of this book examines the agenda and ideal of human progress, finds it in need of revision, and rededicates it to serve the commonwealth of life. Part Two envisions an economics built around stewardship, governments dedicated to trusteeship, and civil societies capable of sustaining human and natural communities. Part Three proposes a new framework for international relations based on the idea of trusteeship and traces the implications of this framework for both domestic and international policies and politics.

Part One reaffirms the goal of human progress understood as the elimination or mitigation of war, famine, brigandage, disease, corrupt authority, and oppressive taxation.[1] The benefits of progress are part of the common heritage of humanity to be shared according to three basic rights. This part argues that in the light of the findings of evolutionary biology – that human beings share many characteristics with the rest of life – moral concerns cannot properly be limited to humans. The almost exclusively human-centered morality that is currently dominant rests upon scientific and metaphysical assumptions that make our relationship to the rest of life mysterious. An alternative idea, 'the commonwealth of life', is described.

Chapter 1, 'Duties Beyond Borders', argues that the ends of universal progress with respect to other humans can best be achieved by respecting three basic rights: bodily integrity; moral, religious, and political choice; and subsistence. It grounds this concern with rights in the desire to preserve ourselves, explicitly recognizes the human propensity toward violence, and universalizes this duty to include all persons. This chapter argues that this conception strikes the best balance between personal liberty and universal duties.

In Chapter 2, 'Duties Beyond the Present and Beyond Persons', it is argued that certain moral concerns that typically apply to persons only must be extended to nonpersons. It begins by arguing that widely shared and fundamental moral principles require the stewardship of both

7

nonrenewable resources and the biosphere for the benefit of future persons. But respect for other lives cannot reasonably be limited to persons. There are no clear, absolute distinctions between ourselves and other species. The characteristics that we find in ourselves are also evident in many other species. We are therefore required to extend to nonpersons certain moral protections that currently apply only or mainly to persons. Differential treatment must be justified by reference to empirical differences and relevant conceptual standards. The alternative to seeing ourselves as part of a continuum with the rest of life is to remain estranged from the universe.

NOTES

1. This list is taken, with modifications, from Barbara Tuchman's *A Distant Mirror*, p. xxx.

CHAPTER 1

DUTIES BEYOND BORDERS

The promises and bargains ... between a Swiss and an Indian, in the woods of America, are binding to them, though they are perfectly in a state of nature in reference to another. For truth and keeping of faith belong to men as men, and not as members of society.

(John Locke, *Two Treatises of Government*)

INTRODUCTION

Several centuries ago, somewhere between the years 1400 and 1500, we began a vast project of improving the human condition. It had antecedents in the civilizations of Egypt, Greece, and Rome and the administrative, scientific and civil orders of India, China, and Japan. But it came with a particular purpose and energy in northern Europe. Out of the plagues, wars, famines, brigandage, unjust taxes, and spiritual crises[1] of the late middle ages there developed a gradual resolve to eliminate or at least mitigate these scourges. The goal of western civilization became to defeat these common enemies.[2]

The instruments were many. The sciences, properly understood and invested in, would yield an understanding of, and a control over, nature that would reduce disease and move us toward food security. Nation states would replace feuding lords who risked the lives and well-being of their vassals as well as their own lives and fortunes. Civil order would be extended over wider realms. Disparate legal systems could give way to a system of law common throughout a nation. The spread of democracy would hold these new governments accountable to their citizens and avoid or at least mitigate the abuse of power: the imposition of unjust taxes, the prosecution of unnecessary wars, and the undue concentration and attendant corruption of power.

In pursuing what I call 'the progress project' it was necessary to control the power of government to prevent abusive use of it, and to use the power of government against the common enemies of humanity. For this reason an adequate theory of government legitimacy was essential. Perhaps the most influential theory of state legitimacy in northern Europe was, and is, that of John Locke, the seventeenth-century English philosopher/physician set out in his *Two Treatises of Government* published about 1690. It has subsequently circled the globe in its influence as the result of the colonial empires of the northern European states. This tendency was carried further as a result of the settlements growing out of a variety of wars, especially the Second World War with the establishment of a western democratic framework in Japan. In this case, grafted to be sure, on a society which rested on markedly different foundations than that of English society in the late 1600s.

Even in the west we have come to doubt many of the assumptions that Locke's theory rested upon. Locke believed that the world and everything in it belonged to God, while in our era religious disbelief and skepticism are more than common. Yet, much of what Locke believed can be supported without belief in God. There are also substantial and growing reasons for doubting much of Locke's account of nature, predating as it did by centuries the development of the atomic theory, the theory of evolution, and the developments of quantum physics. The tradition in which Locke wrote is conceived, in the main, as though humans strode on an empty stage; as if humans had souls and nothing else did. Nevertheless, Locke points the way beyond the confines of his age, and, as we will see, our own.

Two ideas from Locke provide useful starting points for reconstructing an adequate theory of government, and lay a firm foundation for the reconstruction of a progressive, global agenda. (These starting points are the ideas of self-preservation and equality. Locke's idea of stewardship will play a key role in the argument of the next chapter.) This theory will then point the way to a reconstruction in our philosophy of nature; economics, politics, and civil society; and finally – with these elements in hand – an adequate theory of international relations. After these starting points are advanced Locke's idea of the self is contrasted with those from other schools of thought; and finally, the basic-rights conception advanced here is defended against objections.

SELF-PRESERVATION

The problem of finding a starting point for ethics and political philosophy alike is to discern where agreement can begin. Locke's strategy, which I adopt here, is to appeal to the nearly universal idea and experience of self-preservation as the fundamental value. In part, the idea is self-evidently, and directly, empirical. Nearly everyone values his or her own life, and seeks, except in rare circumstances, to extend it. We generally fear death.

From the outset this strategy means that the moral universe includes all persons.

Yet, as Locke recognized, the idea of the self is more complex than it would initially appear. It is tied up in our choices: what we invest in materially and spiritually. Who we are depends on the family we are from, our sense of place, our relations with others. What we value is the conservation of the valuing self: that which specifies what we desire to be. People risk their lives routinely through hazardous activities such as mountain climbing and unhealthy practices such as smoking. These actions are not evidence against the idea of self-preservation so long as these activities are chosen voluntarily. The life of each individual has pre-eminent value to that person since all other values, independent of beliefs about immortality, depend upon continued life. This is not an infinite value since most people are willing to shorten their life expectancies in return for other goods, principles they hold dear, and commitments they have made. Placing a person involuntarily at risk, such as in the military draft, is justified (in the rare cases it is justified) as a necessary sacrifice for the preservation of the lives of other members of the community. Locke thought of government as being legitimated by reference to a hypothetical contract between individuals entered into for self-protection which we seek for ourselves, and which we owe to others. This contract removes individuals from what Locke called the 'state of nature' where each may enforce his or her rights against others in the event of trans-gressions.[3] The state of nature is characterized by certain inconveniences. People will be judges in their own cases and thus not have the requisite impartiality, and they may get carried away by their passions in extracting revenge for the transgressions against them. Locke thus sees government as an essential way of avoiding revenge cycles so characteristic of the civil wars of our era.

There is much in Locke's thought that has been taken to support radical individualism.[4] But this is a very partial reading.[5] Locke's ideas about rights were developed in the context of, and he saw rights as subordinate to, natural law. In writing of the powers of the legislator Locke says:

> The power in the utmost bounds of it, is limited to the public good of the society. The obligations of the law of nature cease not in society ... and have by human laws known penalties annexed to them to enforce their observation. Thus the law of nature stands as an eternal rule to all men, legislators as well as others. The rules that they make ... must ... be conformable to the law of nature, i.e., to the will of God, ... and the fundamental law of nature being the preservation of mankind, no human sanction can be good or valid against it.[6]

We remove ourselves from the state of nature in part to secure our rights and in part to allow us to discharge our natural law duties to others to 'preserve all mankind.' Without going into the intricacies of natural law we can capture the bounded nature of his conception of natural rights by reference to the idea of equality of persons, and that of the stewardship of the commons. Both of these conceptions serve to constrain the exercise of rights, to precede consent. Rights can properly only be exercised 'within the bounds of the law of nature',[7] and this law requires that we equally respect the rights of others. Here is another way in which Locke points us in the right direction. He saw clearly that there could be duties which did not rest on promises, or on actual reciprocity. Our obligations often precede our promises, as opposed to being derived from them. Since no one asks to be born, our obligations to our parents never rest entirely on promises we have made. The contract is not the source of our rights and obligations but the means we choose to protect and discharge them.

EQUALITY

Another fundamental building block in Locke's project to provide a foundation for legitimate authority is the idea of the equality of persons. This claim is almost never a claim that persons are factually equal in intelligence, attractive appearance, drive, and other characteristics with respect to which people obviously differ markedly. As R. H. Tawney argues the idea of equality asserts that:

> [W]hile they differ profoundly as individuals in capacity and character, they are equally entitled as human beings to consideration and respect, and that the well-being of a society is likely to be increased if it so plans its organization that, whether their powers are great or small, all its members may be equally enabled to make the best of such powers as they may possess.[8]

A way to characterize the post-feudal world is as a gradual widening and deepening of the idea of equality of respect for all persons. There were regressions to be sure, massive ones under capitalist, and communist regimes alike. But the underlying tendency remains firmly in place.

The origins of the idea of equality are remote in history. One source is certainly the Old Testament ideas of the Covenant between God and the Hebrew people. All Hebrews were equal before God's judgments. From the grandeur of the divine perspective, differences in life station were irrelevant. In the New Testament the idea that salvation is open to all further emphasizes the fundamental equality of persons. The good Samaritan story implies that all persons are equally entitled to mutual aid independent of their group affiliation. Other distant sources include the Stoic philosophy that the universe is understandable by all rational persons; and Roman ideas that citizenship belongs to all. These ideas come together in the founding of the modern state, most particularly in the

American and French revolutions of approximately two centuries ago.[9]

The spirit of equality is powerfully captured by the Golden Rule: 'do unto others as you would have them do unto you.' This claim takes as fundamental a common humanity among persons over certain basic things. It does not say that all persons should be able to play the cello if one person wants to, but that the choice of what to do should be respected in all. It takes the bodily integrity, ability to choose, and subsistence of each person as fundamental.[10]

Despite the almost certain religious origins of the idea of equality of respect, shared by this author, there are powerful nonreligious arguments as well. Any denial of equality of respect depends upon specifying in what way some are more deserving of respect than others. It is hard, indeed, impossible in my judgment, to find some way of characterizing the relevant differences that is not pernicious. Wealth, social status, or birth circumstances by themselves are irrelevant in determining whether one should be treated with equal respect. Neither race, gender, ethnicity, religion, nationality, nor any of the other characteristics that might be advanced as the basis for unequal treatment, can legitimately count as a rational basis for inequality of respect.

The idea of equality of respect connects in a powerful way with that of self-preservation. For whatever I require on my own behalf about the construction and preservation of my own autonomy applies, if I accept the idea of equality of respect, with similar considerations on the part of others. The idea of the value of one's personal autonomy rests on the same footing as the value of the autonomy of all. The preservation of oneself and the preservation of others are of equal moral worth wherever they may be.

The goal of preserving the valuing self is achieved by respecting the three basic human rights: bodily integrity; religious, moral, and political choice; and subsistence. As Henry Shue has argued in *Basic Rights*, these rights are interlocking and must be satisfied simultaneously. Violence and the palpable fear of violence make a mockery of choice. Without subsistence the other two rights cannot be achieved. Without political choice and the attendant means to hold those who govern accountable we cannot be sure that we receive our due as *rights*. A benevolent dictator might, for example, provide subsistence for the population but then withdraw it on a whim. Means of redress against the government are essential to guarantee the right.[11] Of course, respecting rights, even subsistence rights, may require simply leaving someone alone.

THE SELF

A question that remains is: What self are we seeking to preserve, to treat equally? This is closely related to two other questions: What is our conception of well-being, of the human good? And what duties do persons have to each other to promote each other's well-being? It is useful to contrast the tripartite-rights conception with the answers four other frameworks give to these questions. Each carries with it a conception of the person; they are neo-classical economics; sustainability; capability theories; (and lastly) deep ecology.

NEO-CLASSICAL ECONOMICS

Within neo-classical economics the self is primarily someone who seeks to maximize his or her own utility often through the maximization of consumption opportunities. As an economics text puts it:

> We begin our discussion by looking at the problem facing a typical consumer. Like everyone else, her resources are limited relative to her desires; that is, she does not have enough income or time to consume every commodity that she could possibly want. The theory of consumer choice examines how a person makes sensible decisions in the presence of such scarcity.
>
> Stating the problem this way suggests that three steps are involved in understanding consumer behavior:
>
> 1. We must know what the consumer *wants* to do. Without knowing her preferences for various commodities, we cannot know what a 'good' solution to the problem of scarcity is from her point of view. Thus, we need a representation of consumer tastes.
> 2. We also need to know what the individual *can* do, given her income and the prices she faces. Hence, we must model the constraints imposed on the decision maker by her limited budget.
> 3. The third step is simply putting the consumer's preferences (which show what she wants to do) together with her constraints (which show what she can do). This allows us to determine which feasible choice maximizes her well-being.[12]

In actual applications, the model is often decorated with other values, such as improved health status and education – especially of women. Nevertheless, the core value, the central account of the good, is the improvement of life through increased consumption as measured by disposable income.

The neo-classical account of the person has a number of shortcomings both with respect to the human good and with regard to duties that we owe one another. It has a mistaken account of what motivates us. It ignores much of what we do. It is blind to the essentially relational aspects of human life.

Motivation

Within the neo-classical school it is typically asserted that all behavior can be explained in terms of self-interest. Yet, we know from daily observation that human behavior must have substantial altruistic features if a species with dependent young, such as our own, is to be able to reproduce successfully. This *necessity* of altruism is easily explained within a general evolutionary model by distinguishing between the *selfishness of the gene* and the unavoidable *altruism of the individual*. Genes seek to reproduce themselves (their language is lust) and the behavioral mechanisms of kin selection is the means by which organisms protect those kin, their offspring, who carry their own or in the case of siblings, similar, genes.

Others, like Milton Friedman, claim that the unit of analysis is not the individual but the family: altruism exists but is confined to the family.[13] We know that this isn't true either. In what we regard as pathological cases altruism does not exist in some families. More important for this argument altruism often extends beyond the family to others; examples from fire and rescue squads, the military, and simple protection of each other among workers on the factory floor abound. The altruism that must be present in nature for evolution to work can be expanded through conditioning to include any group as the object of allegiance and sacrifice. In fact, this conditioning was viewed as essential by some of the father figures of the neo-classical world such as John Stuart Mill.[14] These ideas were revived in the 1970s with the concept of interdependent utility functions: where one individual's well-being is seen as dependent on that of another.

The question is not, as the neo-classicist would have it, whether altruism exists. Of course it does. The moral questions before us as individuals and for society is *which* altruism do we want, and which portion of self-interest do we want to reinforce, by which sanction? The answer to these questions, of course, derives from religious and philosophical sources for those who choose to ask them. Evolution by itself provides little guidance on what we *ought* to do.

One way to view the New Testament Good Samaritan story is as an account of the morally appropriate bounds of altruism. Jesus held that in helping the Jew the Samaritan was doing what morality required because the group to whom allegiance and sacrifice is owed is all persons. A characteristic of our own time is that many persons ranging from Albert Schweitzer, to Arne Naess and Aldo Leopold argue that even limiting the universe of caring to persons is too limited because the relevant group is life itself.[15]

Sometimes it is argued that the self-interest model is just a methodological assumption. This argument goes as follows: we know that altruism permeates life, but we have adopted the self-interested assumption in order to show that there are circumstances under which, if all individuals *were* completely selfish, a competitive equilibrium would nevertheless have certain properties that would reasonably be deemed desirable by a disinterested (unselfish) party. For example, all persons pursuing their interests alone are better off through exchange: both the farmer and the consumer are better off through voluntary purchase of corn. Of course, there are a vast number of cases like this, but the assumption is pernicious, not some methodological nicety as the claim implies. This is so because it is often coupled with the claim that the pursuit of self-interest is what constitutes rational behavior. Persons who pay attention to the bonds of community, variously defined, are then perceived to be fools rather than members.

Ignoring much of what we do

Mainstream economics acts as if social life is divided into two parts. First, there is what can be analyzed in the language of economics: trade balances, GNP measures, public goods, externalties, and so on. Second, all other descriptions of human social life are relegated to the realm of tastes or preferences, or treated as marginal. But human life comprises at least four realms: having, doing, being, and relating. Economics describes mostly the first of these, or at least the production and consumption elements of having, and some of relating, for example, competition, negotiating, and contracts, but there is no reason to accede to its neglect of the other realms of human life. Indeed, it is important to see that the neo-classical scheme is an assault on the other three elements.

There are a number of ways that the neo-classical scheme is unsatisfactory with respect to what human beings do. One of the main objectives of the mainstream is the creation of jobs. In the main, this presupposes an industrial model of social organization with set hours and compensation. This increasingly does not describe even our own society, or even the life of neo-classical economists themselves, and is oblivious to the great variety of ways in which production and social life can be arranged.

From the mainstream point of view many people in the world are poor, as we can see from their low incomes. But this viewpoint presupposes a money economy. As the neo-classicists try to reduce poverty by increasing income they often destroy other ways of life where money did not play a central role, and which provided for human well-being in other terms.

For the mainstream a healthy economy aims at increasing productivity, where productivity is defined as extra units of output per unit of input: labor and capital. If this regime ever achieved its goals we would all be out of work. As this scheme partially succeeds it leaves people as marginal to the economy with no compensating mechanism of distribution, and, as we will see in Chapter 3, relies on a conceptual scheme that more and more erodes existing safeguards for those unable to function in an economy.

Work is not always unpleasant and something we do only so that we can have leisure and consume, as is often claimed. At best this generalizes from a subset of jobs to all jobs. In many cases it reverses the relationship between work and consumption – where we consume in order to work. For many, work is the essence of life and not necessarily related to an end.

Relating

Neo-classical economists also typically claim that human well-being is automatically increased by well-functioning markets, with high substitutability, productivity gains and perfect capital and labor mobility. But this is true neither of the family nor the firm.[16] The Brownian motion of a perfectly mobile labor force – with workers moving to the best-paying job wherever it is – is incompatible with the maintenance of family or of the organization and other embedded role/status relationships. This is but a symptom of the failure of this school of thought to offer any explicit account at all of what persons owe one another beyond the characteristics of fair exchange.[17]

SUSTAINABLE DEVELOPMENT

This school of thought gained considerable credence after the Brundtland Report *Our Common Future*.[18] Nearly everyone who writes or works in the field of international development, and more and more even in discussions of 'advanced' economies, feels obligated to acknowledge the importance of the idea of sustainability. It is defined in the Brundtland report as follows:

> Sustainable development is development that meets the needs of the present without compromising the ability of future generations to meet their own needs. It contains within it two key concepts:
>
> - the concept of 'needs,' in particular the essential needs of the world's poor, to which overriding priority should be given; and
> - the idea of limitations imposed by the state of technology and social organization on the environment's ability to meet present and future needs.[19]

Sustainability can be thought of as a very generalized conception of duties to treat all generations equally. It is a distinct improvement over the neo-classical school for two reasons. First, it is not committed to discounting (assigning a lower value to events in the future) since it explicitly puts the needs of every generation on the same footing. In contrast, the neo-classical insistence on discounting, as we will see in Chapter 3 – at least implicitly treats the future as of significantly less value than the present. Second, it has some way of prioritizing among consumption opportunities, which the neo-classicist does not, in concentrating on the satisfaction of needs, particularly those of the poor. This is similar to the tripartite-rights-conception concern with subsistence.

The sustainability school thus offers some account of duties, but often has no clear conception of the good. Even Herman Daly's work, one of its most articulate proponents, contains at least two tendencies that pull in divergent directions. On the one hand he remains entangled in the neo-classical web of the good in making consumption its main objective. For instance, Daly talks of shortage of 'natural' capital, for example, fish, as being more of a limiting factor than human-made capital, for example, fishing boats.[20] But the controlling goal is still human consumption. This weakens the claim considerably because it is unclear, just to take Daly's example, that the *consumption* function of fish cannot be substituted by other sources of protein, or by a vegetarian diet. The point would be better grounded, even within an anthropocentric ethic, by pointing to the *employment* effects of resource depletion and to the shortage of sinks for waste disposal than by focusing merely on the consumption dimensions. Nevertheless, it is promising to call into question the neo-classical insistence on complete resource substitution. In this way the sustainability school opens up discourse on a crucial issue.

Daly has a richer and more adequate conception of the person than he deploys in this argument. For example, the conception of person-in-community set out in his book with John Cobb *For the Common Good*[21] emphasizes the social and interdependent characteristics of human relations. This idea opens up a promising (old) avenue of thought that enriches the conception of the person considerably, and suggests criteria by which to judge forms of production and consumption. For example, the idea of person-in-community provides a powerful antidote to the idea of highly mobile labor markets.

Despite the more promising conception of the person embedded in the writings of authors like Daly, much of the sustainability school, which might be called neo-classical sustainability, remains open to the many criticisms of the neo-classical conception of the person; that is, not having an account of the person that includes doing, being and having. In addition, also like the neo-classical conception, it offers no account of which consumption is desirable beyond the satisfaction of needs. This is part of a general problem with current conceptions of sustainable development, perhaps because much of the work grows out of the biological and physical sciences, and economics; none of which are accustomed to giving ethical arguments: they offer little illumination on the question of what *should*, on principle, be sustained.

CAPABILITY THEORIES

A robust conception of the human well-being *is* presented in the capabilities literature, which is one of the areas of work of Nobel Laureate Amartya Sen. It points to a set of generic human capacities that should be the goal of development and good societies generally, and serves as an essential corrective to the poverty of the neo-classical conception of the person. The main idea is that each person should be capable of those functionings which are necessary for human flourishing; for example, exercise, a family (or at least sexual) life, intellectual and artistic expression, and the like. As David Crocker puts it:

> Capabilities theorists choose valuable human 'functionings' and capabilities to function as the basis of their ethical outlook. They argue that these moral categories are superior to other candidates for *fundamental* concepts, such as resources or commodities, utilities, needs, or rights ... What do capabilities theorists mean by the term *functionings*? A person's functionings consist of his or her physical and mental states ('beings') and activities ('doings'). The most important of these functionings, the failure of which constitutes poverty and the occurrence of which constitutes well-being, 'vary from such elementary physical ones as being well-nourished, being adequately clothed and sheltered, avoiding preventable morbidity, and so forth, to more complex social achievements such as taking part in the life of the community, being able to appear in public without shame, and so on.' A person's *capabilities* are that set of functionings open to the person, given the person's personal characteristics ('endowment') as well as economic and social opportunities.[22]

This advances the discussion beyond the neo-classical and related sustainability schools by not embracing discounting and offering a more complex account of what should be sustained. Yet, as it stands today the capability literature is truncated at best when compared to an adequate theory of the person.

This is so for at least four reasons, the first related to the conception of the good, the last three to the issues of duties. First, the list of capabilities is long, sometimes as many as a dozen dimensions are listed, yet no standard of choice is presented for what to do when there is conflict between them. Conceptually, then, one will be unable to find guidance about what to do just when it may be most needed. If the neo-classical school can be criticized for having too few, or even one indicator of success, GDP per capita, then the capabilities school can be cited for having too many. It is too complicated.

Second, though this school of thought contains a theory of the good person, it provides no account of obligations to produce the good. It is understandable that Aristotle – the historical source of much of this school of thought – provides only partial answers to this question because he presupposes an intact, functioning community with clear duties. Yet without some account of what humans owe one another there is no reason to see why one should care at all about others. As a philosophy of development *assistance,* the sustainability school implies a universal duty to assist all persons in the world to flourish. But this requires too much. There is no *duty* on the part of the Norwegians, for example, to help build opera houses in Haiti.

A third and related difficulty is that the capability school also presents little in the way of institutional context. Though David Crocker's work is somewhat of an exception to this, there is little in the way of an account of civil society, a key element in the construction of the self in this school of thought. Nor does it contain an explicit philosophy of governance, so the human self seemingly floats free of the various circumstances that give it shape. This is also true of its vision of the place of the human self in nature. This is the fourth difficulty. It lacks a philosophy of nature. It provides no answer to the question of what the relationship is between human well-being and the well-being of other species, except perhaps as instrumental to human flourishing.

The capabilities school of thought is at once too broad and too narrow. It is too broad in presenting a diffuse account of the good, and too narrow in not presenting an account of duties or the institutional structure that the account of the self presupposes. In these last two respects it is similar to the school of thought it proports to replace: neo-classical economics. It substitutes a bigger keyhole for the narrow one given by the neo-classical school, but it is a keyhole nonetheless.

THE TRIPARTITE-RIGHTS-BASED CONCEPTION

The rights-based conception that I argue for contains three rights, each of which must be satisfied. These rights are rights of bodily integrity, rights of moral, political and religious choice, and subsistence rights.[23] The case for a rights-based conception can be set out by reference to the defects of these other schools we have just considered.

Tripartite Rights Contrasted with Capability

There is no priority among the three rights, though they trump all other moral considerations, except in very extreme circumstances.[24] Each of the three rights clusters must be simultaneously achieved/protected for a society to be just and for development to be successful. Yet the desideratum is much more conceptually and operationally tractable than the capabilities list. Three interlocking rights replace up to a dozen unprioritized objectives.

In addition, the tripartite-rights conception offers an account of who is responsible for what, and at least some account of the institutional structure that its view presupposes. At first this might not appear to be the case. For rights claims are forbearance and assistance claims against *all* other persons and thus might appear to be both unfocused and overreaching. Here is where the conception of government as trustee and the idea of a robust civil society play crucial roles.

Each government is the ultimate, though by no means the proximate, guarantor of the three basic rights. It is not proximate because it is the duty of each person to respect the rights of all others, buttressed and directed by a civil society. It is individuals who have the duties in the first place. It is the duty of government to see that these obligations are discharged by those within its borders toward others within its borders. It is the duty of other governments and global civil society to assist those governments that cannot, and to sanction those governments which do not, discharge these most fundamental obligations. There is thus a nested set of duties which can be depicted as follows:

1. All persons have obligations to respect the basic rights of all other persons.
2. Governments have default obligations to enforce and/or execute themselves the obligations of individuals when individuals fail to discharge them.
3. The international community has the default obligations to enforce and/or execute these obligations when nations fail to discharge them.

Tripartite Rights Contrasted with Sustainability

A rights conception welcomes the at least implicit rejection of discounting that is contained in the idea of sustainable development. But it is more robust than the sustainability school in offering a more complex account of what *should* be sustained: namely, those human institutions and natural processes necessary for satisfying the three basic rights indefinitely into the future. The tripartite conception of rights avoids the narrow conception of the person as consumer that the sustainability school, at least in some versions, shares with neo-classical economics. The conception of the person is broad enough to provide a foundational account of human life.

This rights conception also opens the door to a much more adequate discussion of the issue of resource substitution than the sustainability school. The tools available to the sustainability school to argue against input substitutions are only, or at least mainly, depending on which school one is discussing, that running out of a resource will limit consumption. The rights conception does not suffer from such a unnecessarily limited portfolio of argument. For example, since its theory of the person places moral, religious, and political choice at the core of its conception, one may argue that the natural world can be an object of these choices, and should be preserved for those reasons, which are not reducible to consumption as normally understood.

Tripartite Rights Contrasted with Neo-classical

The three-way rights conception contains a more neutral conception of the goal of policy than the neo-classical school. It is more robust in the preservation of cultures. Rather than define the problem of development as one of poverty elimination to be solved by more income, the rights conception focuses on the means of the preservation of life. In many cases this may require little or no intervention in the lives of traditional peoples. By contrast, the neo-classical conception is inherently interventionist. By insisting on improvements in *income* it assures the destruction of cultures not based on a money economy. The more integrated the world's peoples become in the global economy the more battered they are by the centrifugal forces of that economy. This assures that the principles of redistribution (each group caring for its own vulnerable), reciprocity (a rough equality of exchange), and householding (production for a limited group) characteristic of healthy societies will be undercut. Then follows closely urban migration and loss of traditional culture and roles. The rights conception helps us to avoid even starting down this unhappy road.

Besides subsistence, the other two clusters of rights also direct our attention to the political dimensions of development. Rights to bodily integrity protect persons against torture, imprisonment without due process, and call attention to the fundamentals of judicial processes. The requirements of moral, religious, and political choice set education for citizenship and the development of democratic institutions at the core of the development process. The three clusters of rights together as the foundation for a conception of development avoids the *ad hoc* 'grafting on' of these concerns that characterizes the neo-classical conception at its best. It thus allows us to say what we mean from the beginning.

Tripartite Rights Contrasted with Deep Ecology

For all the strengths of the rights-based conception we cannot be completely content with Locke's formulation of it. Human co-evolution with the rest of life is an unavoidable fact. As our understanding of our desires and even our metabolism becomes clearer it is apparent that we are one with nature in a way that Locke's at least implicit view of humans as belonging to a higher order than the rest of nature (derivative of the doctrine of special creation – the idea that humans were specially created by God) is unwarranted. Rather, than being an independent rights holder separate from nature, human beings are 'osmotic' with respect to nature. In his *Ecology, community and lifestyle* Arne Naess points to what I call the 'osmotic self.'[25] He emphasizes that we are in continuous material, emotional, and spiritual interchange with our environment. He speaks of the transcendental *S*elf which differs from the empirical self of consciousness. In his introduction to this volume of Naess's work translator David Rothenberg states:

> Naess's use of Self-realisation is a bold attempt to connect the general statement that 'all life is fundamentally one' with our individual needs and desires ... I here ... mention several points to alleviate misunderstanding.
>
> 1. Self-realization is not self-centered. Remember the capital S, but at the same time do not think the individual self or ego is dissolved in the larger Self. The diversity of different individuals and approaches remains, as we share and shape our connections to the larger...
>
> 2. If one really expands oneself to include other people and species and nature itself, altruism becomes unnecessary. The larger world becomes part of our own interests. It is seen as a world of *potentials* to increase our own Self-realization as we are part of the increase of others'.
>
> 3. The word in Norwegian is Selv-realisering: Self-realising. It is an active condition, not a place one can reach. No one ever reaches Self-realization, for complete Self-realisation would require the realisation of all. Just as no one in certain Buddhist traditions ever reaches nirvana, as the rest of the world must be pulled along to get there. It is only a process, a way to live one's life.[26]

The reported experiences of oneness with the rest of life have a strong affinity with a great variety of reports of mysticism from the world's religions, and no doubt would have been a familiar idea to Locke himself.

This account of the oneness with nature does not, however, count as a reason to abandon Locke's rights-grounded conception of the person. For the osmotic account, though true, can go too far, person in community, person in nature, it does not matter since it is clearly still *person* in ... some thing. If we accept the osmotic Self as central and a complete description then all distinctive aspects of the person disappear along with all responsibility *to* the self or Self, and all responsibility *of* the self/Self. The person completely disappears into nature, and our responsibility for it, and for each other, with it. By dint of the great power we have over other persons and the rest of nature the question of human responsibility is overwhelmingly acute at this point in history, and dwarfs any sense of proto-responsibility in other creatures. The rights conception thus fixes human responsibility in a world otherwise described largely in terms of relational fields. The rights conceptions serve to protect the individual self/Self, and to provide a tractable account of, and locus for, obligation.

OBJECTIONS TO THE TRIPARTITE-RIGHTS CONCEPTION

The three-way rights conception can be objected to for at least four reasons. First, that it takes a specific north Atlantic conception of the person and our relations to each other and universalizes it to cultures that do not share its premises. Second, that it tends to undercut certain socially desirable behavior because it supports radically individualistic behavior. Third, that it requires either too much or too little sacrifice. And fourth, that it is such an abstract and legalistic conception that it neglects what motivates people to care for one another.

MORAL IMPERIALISM

The three-way conception of rights is not shared by all cultures. Indeed, the language of rights in any form is foreign to some cultures. The idea of a minimal set of rights coupled with sometimes indirect, but nevertheless universal, duties may be thought therefore to constitute a sort of moral imperialism: the willingness to force a conception that arose in one part of the world, at a particular time, on all the world. The whole project of a world ethic may be suspect. Indeed, cosmopolitan ethics, it can be argued, may be a screen – knowingly or unknowingly – for imperialism.

Though it is true that the explicit language of rights does not exist in all cultures, it is meaningful to describe relations in all cultures with these words. In many cultures what one person owes another is derived from the roles they hold. For example, we know what is owed the parishioner from describing the role of the priest. What children are entitled to can be filled in by describing their role and that of the parent, siblings, extended family and the like. In societies with stable role relations the language of rights is unnecessary. We can say what people owe one another without it, but we can also describe these role relations with the language of rights if we so choose.

But once role relations become destabilized the language of *human* rights becomes necessary, for the role is no longer stable enough to describe who owes what to whom. It was the breakdown of the European feudal order in the sixteenth and seventeenth centuries that initially gave birth to the rights language. The causes of this collapse were multiple. The rise of the market opened up somewhat isolated towns to trade. The hegemony of the church was challenged. Religious wars raged. Technology changed from ways to keep time, to farm, and to print. The old, slowly changing order was swept away. Modernity became the next stage of history.

Rights language thus describes what one owes to another under conditions of role instability. It serves a parallel function in cases of multiple roles. Where people have multiple roles in work, family, and community the language of human rights serves to simplify what is owed as a minimum to a person as a human independent of those roles. We can describe, therefore, the relations among people in a variety of cultures using the language of rights. Indeed, as the world moves toward economic globalization under the trading states model, traditional roles are destabilized, and rights language becomes more and more necessary to describe who is owed what. The need for moral structure explains why rights language arises, and why it is gaining great currency around the world. My argument above has been that the only adequate conception of rights has to be the three-way conception, for operationally each right entails the other. Once rights language gets underway we are led inexorably to the three basic rights, including the right to choice.

The development of a minimum set of global standards based on rights will have revolutionary consequences for the world's cultures, perhaps none are more revolutionary than to change the status of women. It seems best in taking on the moral imperialism charge to take on a hard case, a case that would entail substantial revisions in the cultures where current practices were set aside: that of female circumcision. The basic-rights conception is gender neutral. The right of bodily integrity rules out circumcision of women below the age of consent, for example. Widely practiced in many cultures circumcision permanently reduces a woman's ability to receive pleasure from sexual experiences. (The right of bodily integrity also raises questions about male circumcision below the age of consent, though with less force since the practice is far less influential on later sexual experience, and also has a limited public health rationale.) The changed sexual status of women that will flow from stopping the practice of circumcision will have profound influences on family life, and thus on those cultures generally. More important perhaps is the changed social status of women that would flow from a recognition that they have equal rights with men. There is no avoiding this implication of the rights conception. Indeed, it is a strength of the language of rights that it can provide an absolute constraint on certain practices. Of course, female infanticide is also ruled out.

The right to moral and political choice is also likely to have profound implications on many cultures as it requires at least rough equality in education between boys and girls concerning basic literacy in mathematics, reading, and writing. This will in turn play out in changing the adult relations between men and women affecting all aspects of social life, as women may then assume nontraditional roles. It thus will strengthen other changes in social structure, some of which are already underway as a result of economic integration.

A distinct strength of the rights conception is its thinness. Once the duties associated with rights have been discharged there is ample room for the expression of cultural particularity. Indeed, there is room for some cultural variety within the rights conception since there is flexibility in how each right is specified within cultures. It is therefore compatible with differing conceptions of what is good for men and women. Its imperialism is thus limited. Moreover, the idea that human rights define a moral minimum has been ratified by the vast majority of the nations of the world in the form of the UN Declaration of Human Rights. If it is imperialism, it has been voluntarily accepted by many.

THE TYRANNY OF INDIVIDUALISM

The rights conception can also be criticized as being too individualistic and legalistic, of ignoring the social bonds that make human life possible to begin with, through mating and the evolution of families, and through the rich cultural life that sets the bounds of acceptable human conduct. It is blind, it could be argued, to the particularities of human culture; to the ties that bind. This is a telling criticism, particularly reflecting on the way the rights conception has actually been played out historically. Much attention has been called to the role of rights as constraints on the actions of others, and on the role of the state; while slighting the duties that are an absolutely integral part of the rights conception. In the United States, for example, there is much focus on the alleged rights of landowners, and little attention paid to the duties that go with the ownership of property: to prevent harm to the property of others, to manage property in a way that recognizes its role in supporting the diversity of life, and so on.

But these defects are not inherent in the rights conception itself. For every right that one person has others also hold a similar right. Reciprocal duties are therefore foundational. For every right that one person has to enjoy his or her liberty so does another, and these specify the duties that go with the rights. A healthy society is not a collection of property rights holders alone, but a balance between a civil order, fiduciary governments, and a robust but appropriately constrained market. It is the balance of powers doctrine writ large.

TOO MUCH OR TOO LITTLE?

Other objections to the rights conception go in opposite directions. It might be held that it requires too much. The universal claims associated with these rights make all accountable to all. People in distant lands can make a claim on citizens of other countries to protect any of their three rights. It would seem that these claims would undercut the ability of those capable of assistance in setting their own goals, in exercising their own moral, political, and religious choices.

To some degree it is true that the rights conception can require people in distant lands to alter their behavior and expectations. But it is not an undue burden. First, any moral system sets some boundary on the pursuit of one's own interests. So the complaint that there is a restriction on the pursuit of interests applies with no particular force to the rights conception. Second, the protection of these rights, as Locke saw so clearly, is one of the reasons that we enter into government to begin with. We set up institutions, particularly governments and charities, to discharge these obligations, so the duties are most commonly discharged indirectly. Our duties are either to assist those in need directly, as the good Samaritan did, or to set up, guide, and finance those institutions that can act on our behalf. At the conclusion of this book a framework for thinking about international relations is set forth that depicts how these duties work.

It might be objected from the opposite perspective that the rights conception requires too little. This could particularly be the case with regard to subsistence. It seems to authorize a world in which some live rather poorly, while others consume large amounts of resources. There are a number of responses to be made to this.

First, the strength of the objection depends on what we take subsistence to mean. I take it to require: adequate nutrition, clean water and air, decent housing and clothing, and basic medical care. Bringing all persons up to minimal levels with respect to these goods would be a substantial departure from the status quo. Second, the conception of stewardship economics defended in Chapter 3 sets us on course for an economic system in which resource consumption would be reduced, and/ or where there would be substantial substitution for current resource use. Third, there needs to be a boundary on obligation. Living a moral life requires that we are able to set our own goals free, to some degree, of the claims of others. Once basic rights are satisfied, the better off may do what they wish subject to the ecological constraints discussed in subsequent chapters. In this way the good Samaritan story strikes the right balance. It tells us what we owe to others, and makes it clear that we may also continue our own journey.

MOTIVATION

Last, it might be objected that the rights conception lacks an account of why people actually care for each other. It is the ties of community and family that motivate sacrifice; reconstructing the neighbor's home destroyed by a tornado, sitting through the night at the hospital bedside of a dying friend, digging into retirement funds to pay for an education for a child, and the like. There is no question that these intimate and/or face-to-face relations are a major part of the picture, but they are not all of it.

This is so for a number of reasons. First, the rights conception lies at the basis of geographically vast, and ethnically diverse, polities such as the United States and Canada. As has been noted already, it is widely recognized in international agreements that these universal obligations exist even beyond the boundaries of nations. These conceptions of rights go beyond the obligations that we have to intimates. Second, the rights conception is not a substitute for more intimate obligations. On the contrary, it defines a minimal set of obligations and freedoms that allows the ties that bind to flourish in the first place. As Locke saw centuries ago, without these moral minimums we are at the mercies of king and compatriot alike to take from us what they can, to do with us what they like. In a just world to keep the home fires burning bright and safe means respecting rights on distant shores.

NOTES

1. See Barbara Tuchman's *A Distant Mirror*, p. xxx.
2. In our time the agenda of progress has come under attack from a variety of sources. The wars, the destruction of nature, and the abuse of power rampant in the twentieth century are widely cited as examples of how the project of progress has run amok. Others question its philosophical and conceptual foundations, predicting its further erosion. Books skeptical of the robustness of the idea of progress include Christopher Lasch's *The True and Only Heaven*, Robert Nelson' *Reaching for Heaven on Earth*, Robert Nisbet's *History of the Idea of Progress*. Also, of course, Dr Theodore Seuss Geisel's *The Lorax*.

   I argue in this book that accounts of the death of progress are premature. What is needed is a firm philosophical footing beginning with a conception of three basic human rights and a redefinition of our place in nature; a re-direction of the institutions of markets, government, and civil society; and a new conception of the relations between nations. As J. B. Bury states in his seminal *The Idea of Progress*, progress is the organizing idea of our civilization. I concur in this assessment, but endeavor to unhook it from a disfunctional economics.
3. John Locke, *Two Treatises of Government*, *Second Treatise*, ch. 2.
4. Scholars who emphasize the radical individualism inherent in Locke are C. B. MacPherson, *The Theory of Possessive Individualism*, Richard Epstein, *Takings*, and Robert Nozick, *Anarchy, State, and Utopia*.
5. See Richard Ashcraft's *Revolutionary Politics and Locke's Two Treatises of Government*, for a discussion of how Locke's theory of natural rights is restrained by his theory of natural law.
6. John Locke, *Two Treatises of Government*, *Second Treatise*, ch. 11, para. 135.
7. John Locke, ibid., ch. 1, para. 4.
8. R. H. Tawney, *The Idea of Equality* quoted from *The Idea of Equality*, edited by George L. Abernathy, p. 233.
9. These ideas are drawn in part from Abernathy's introduction to *The Idea of Equality*.
10. See Rawl's distinction between primary and secondary goods, John Rawls, *A Theory of Justice*, pp. 92–5.

11. Henry Shue, *Basic Rights*.

12. Michael L. Katz and Harvey S. Rosen, *Microeconomics*, p. 22.

13. Milton Friedman, *Capitalism and Freedom*, p. 12.

14. John Stuart Mill, *Utilitarianism* in John Stuart Mill and Jeremy Bentham, *Utilitarianism and Other Essays*, p. 278 and p. 286.

15. Keith Thomas, *Man and the Natural World: A History of the Modern Sensibility* and James Rachels, *Created from Animals: The Moral Implications of Darwinism*. Also see John Cobb's suggestion that there are degrees of intrinsic value related to capacity to feel, John Cobb, 'Ecology, Ethics, and Theology,' in Herman E. Daly and Kenneth Townsend (eds), *Valuing the Earth: Economics, Ecology, Ethics*.

16. See Edith Penrose, *The Theory of the Growth of the Firm*.

17. Edith Stokey and Richard Zeckhauser, *A Primer for Policy Analysis*.

18. World Commission on Environment and Development, *Our Common Future*.

19. Ibid., p. 43.

20. See, for example, Herman E. Daly, *Beyond Growth: The Economics of Sustainable Development*, p. 78.

21. Herman E. Daly and John B. Cobb, Jr., *For the Common Good*, pp. 159–75.

22. David A. Crocker, 'Hunger, Capability, and Development' in William Aiken and Hugh LaFollette (eds), *World Hunger and Mortality*, pp. 219–20. Alternative points of view about this school of thought can be found in Amartya Sen, 'Gender Inequality' in Martha Nussbaum and Jonathan Glover (eds), *Women, Culture and Development: A Study of Human Capabilities*, and Martha Nussbaum, 'The Good As Discipline, As Freedom' in David A. Crocker and Toby Linden (eds), *Ethics of Consumption: The Good Life, Justice, and Global Stewardship*, pp. 318–20.

23. The scope of each of these rights needs to be specified in a fully developed theory: the way in which bodily integrity limits pollution, the limits to choice, and the scope of subsistence rights. Such an account will help specify what to do in cases where the rights conflict; e.g. conflicts between reproduction rights based on religious liberty, versus subsistence rights and duties to preserve the common heritage of humankind.

24. For instance, rights of civil assembly might be curtailed in the cases of clear and present danger of riot and looting. Of course, exceptions like these can be subject to abuse; but that is not a reason for not stating them.

25. Arne Naess, *Ecology, community and lifestyle: Outline of an Ecosophy*.

26. Ibid., p. 9.

CHAPTER 2

DUTIES BEYOND THE PRESENT AND BEYOND PERSONS

> Man with all his noble qualities, with sympathy which feels for the most debased, with benevolence which extends not only to other men but to the humblest living creature, with his god-like intellect which has penetrated into the movements and constitution of the solar system – with all these exalted powers – Man still bears in his bodily frame the indelible stamp of his lowly origin.
>
> (Charles Darwin, *The Descent of Man*)

Equality of respect is a principle that extends across space. Whether located in Japan or Turkey, all persons are to be accorded a fundamental equality of respect. Once the idea of equality is joined to the right of self-preservation the moral significance of space is flattened. All persons have presumptive claims to equal moral standing. Simply being at a distance itself makes no difference. This is a fundamental feature of a cosmopolitan ethic.

Of course, there are a number of ways that the obligations that go with rights can be discharged. Distance may be correlated with factors that do make a difference, that do have moral relevance, a distant problem may be the responsibility of another government, another family, or another person. Equal respect for all, expressed through respecting the three basic rights, is a default principle that comes into play when these other factors cannot be counted upon. For example, if a parent abuses his or her child we recognize that there is a collective responsibility to protect the child because those who have first-order responsibility are not discharging it.

STEWARDSHIP

Stewardship simply extends the principle of equal respect through time. Just as we take spatial location as irrelevant in moral claims based on equality of respect, so should a person's location in time be considered irrelevant. Being born in 1900, 2000, or 2100 is irrelevant from a moral point of view. Of course, as is the case with spatial location distance in time may be correlated with factors that are relevant. The further in the future it is that an event may occur the less sure we may be about whether it will occur at all or what its characteristics may be. People who live in the future may be richer than we are, and hence their subsistence rights may be more secure, thus lessening our responsibility. Or we may think that they will be worse off due to resource shortages, climate change, or civil disorder, thus creating obligations to avoid or mitigate these consequences. But particular location in time is irrelevant. The cosmopolitan duties of a world ethic apply through both space and time.

Locke argued that we may take from the commons as long as there is 'enough and as good for others.' This is the famous Lockean proviso. There is no reason to think that the restriction in the proviso would apply only to persons who live in the present. But this is not only a prohibition against harm to present or future persons. What I am advancing is a more controversial reading of Locke than simply avoidance of harm, what Nigel Dower has called a more generous interpretation.[1] The proviso goes beyond avoiding harm to others to seeing the appropriation of, or from, the commons as entailing positive duties. Those who wish to interpret this as avoidance of harm only, such as Robert Nozick in *Anarchy, State and Utopia*, use it to ground the idea of natural rights to property. They neglect altogether the feature of Locke's natural *law* argument that requires the 'preservation' of all humankind.

The ultimate rationale for private appropriation of the commons is that it serve the common good. As Richard Ashcraft notes in *Revolutionary Politics and Locke's Two Treatises of Government*:

> It is quite true that ... under this view, particular individuals may be able to acquire considerable wealth as the outcome of their productive and beneficial actions, but to suggest that Locke ever sets men free from their natural law obligations such that wealth may be accumulated solely because individuals desire to do so and without social constraints on its employment is to reverse completely the thrust of his argument in the *Second Treatise*...[2]

On the fiduciary conception land is not something that can be used simply for the benefit of the present owner, but an asset that must be used for the common good understood in a multi-generational context. It is a community resource. As we will see in Chapter 5 this view is compatible with the private ownership of real property, but rights of the owner come with the responsibilities of a steward. Private ownership, capital, and market institutions have their place, but in a larger fiduciary/stewardship framework.

There are a number of elements buried in the concept of stewardship. It originates in the Anglo-Saxon idea of 'stig-weard' – the keeper of the hall; one who cares for and improves the hall. In its original meaning the steward is one who cuts the wood, tends the fire, lays aside the timbers for the next time the roof needs repair. A steward is thus one who looks after something on behalf of another; who cares for what he has been en*trusted* with. Hence the idea that stewardship is a *trust*. There is something to be cared for, someone from whom the asset is secured, and someone, perhaps the person who gave the asset or someone else, for whose benefit it is managed. In Locke's world the something to be cared for was the global commons: in his view the unenclosed lands of England and America. The giver was God, who regarded the world – we are told in Genesis – as good; the beneficiaries were humanity. Humanity is thus God's guardian of the earth on behalf of this and future generations.

In Locke's view, common property resources could be appropriated as long as the benefits of the appropriation were widely shared with the beneficiaries. The common pasture lands of England could be enclosed if it could be shown that it would increase the food supply for all. This is one of many strokes of genius in Locke's theory. He gets from the world as given by God to humankind in common, perhaps from Psalms,[3] to the institution of private property by showing that private property serves the beneficiaries of the trust. Of course, the institution of private property is a success in precisely this way. At the time of Locke's writings the population of England was about five million people and threatened with chronic food shortages, but normally not famine.[4] Today even with fifty-five million people and millions of acres of prime farmland converted to urban uses, Britain is a net food exporter! Seen as a means of discharging what Locke took to be our natural-law obligations to 'preserve all mankind,' the institution of private property, along with a number of other factors in the productive success of modern agriculture, is a runaway success. Simply put, private property, subject to proper constraints, is one of the best ideas ever.

It has been argued that this conception of stewardship is a tidy picture as long as God is in it.[5] But, so the argument continues, in a time when faith in God can no longer easily be assumed, the conception unravels. For there is no giver of the asset to be cared for, and no one on whose behalf the steward acts. This point does not have the fatal consequences normally supposed. For one thing, hundreds and hundreds of millions of people around the world in the Judeo-Christian-Islamic tradition, and in other traditions, do believe the original story or something like it. For them Locke's world of God the giver, and humanity the guardian is more or less intact. But what about those who do not believe in God, or anything of the kind?

Can they accept stewardship? Can they believe in caring for things on behalf of others as a foundational principle of morality? An alternative, nontheologically based, grounding of the idea of stewardship can be found in the idea of role reciprocity; already set forth in our discussion of the idea of equality in the previous chapter: do unto others as you would have them do unto you. Actual reciprocity is not required by this rule, otherwise there would not be obligations to children, the infirm, or the terminally ill. We would owe nothing to those who cannot reciprocate. Yet we take our obligations to the vulnerable to be among the most fundamental. This is how the golden rule can ground our obligations to future generations of humans and, as we are about to see, to all of life without a theological basis. We should treat others as we would like to be treated if we were in their circumstances.

Stewardship is a form of thought and feeling that one can adopt within the world. It is a recognition that there are appropriate limits to the expression and satisfaction of one's own desires. As noted in the discussion of Naess in the previous chapter, the self that throbs with appetite and desire is but a part of who we are. There is also the ability to step back from this where the Self becomes merged with the larger community of persons and ultimately, as we will see in the next section, of life. We can take the well-being of others who are in our own country and those who are citizens of foreign lands into account. Those who share our historical era and those who do not. As John Rawls says in the last sentence of *A Theory of Justice*: 'Purity of heart, if one could attain it, would be to see clearly and to act with grace and self-command from this point of view.'[6] Stewardship is an act of caring for ourselves, the beneficiaries of the trust, and others in the present and through time.

THE COMMONWEALTH OF LIFE

The ideas of equality and stewardship are customarily taken to express duties toward other persons only. As long as there are relevant moral differences between persons and the rest of nature this boundary is appropriate. But painful as many of us find our demotion from lord to mere member of the world these differences can no longer be maintained. The empirical evidence that we share an ancestry with other animals is overwhelming, as is the evidence that many of the things that we once took as special about ourselves (most commonly the ability to reason) are found – often in abundance – throughout nature.

Many of the arguments we use to justify the preservation of nature treat the problem as one of justifying how we treat something different from us; something which belongs to a different order of being. This is a likely holdover from the doctrine of special creation that saw humans as the only creature made in the image of God. Some of these arguments presume we are spectators, others that we have only instrumental relations to the rest of life. These include the need to preserve sources of DNA for pharmaceutical drugs, the cleansing features of natural systems with respect to air and water, the beauty of nature, nature as the handiwork of God, keystone arguments (that we had better leave things alone because we don't know what will happen if we dis-equilibrate systems), and transformative value arguments (that we need the experience of nature for our own spiritual renewal).

There is considerable value to each of these arguments, and I wish to discard none of them. When coupled with the idea of equality through time, these arguments provide an anthropocentric ground for stewardship of nature. Each generation should pass on to its successors the abilities to benefit from nature that it enjoyed. Further, since nature provides a great variety of benefits, including being the object of aesthetic appreciation and religious worship, its diversity must be preserved. This broader interpretation of our relationship to nature serves to block the idea that it is only nature's directly productive capacities such as forest and farm that are of interest to future persons.

Nevertheless, there is a more fundamental set of issues at stake, grounded in both the Judeo-Christian and ancient Greek sources of morality. These are, respectively, the golden rule and the requirement that equals be treated equally. Similar ideas can also be supported by Buddhist ideas of universal compassion.[7]

THE GOLDEN RULE

As noted above, the golden rule is a role reciprocity rule, not a strict reciprocity rule. In traditional morality it is taken to apply to persons only because of the doctrine of special creation – that human beings are unique because we have been created in the image of God.

JUSTICE AS TREATING EQUALS EQUALLY

This is normally taken to apply to persons only for two reasons. One is the inherent narcissism of the underlying question: what is the *human* good? Albert Schweitzer argues correctly in *The Philosophy of Civilization* that:

> The process by which Western thought has hitherto sought for a world view is doomed to be fruitless. It has consisted simply in interpreting the world in the sense of world- and life-affirmation, that is to say, in attributing to the world a meaning which allows it to conceive the aims of mankind and of individual men as having a meaning within that world.[8]

Beginning with the idea that the problem to be solved, the interpretation to be sought, was the meaning of *human* life is the step that has set western civilization on the road of regarding the rest of nature as an after-thought. Second, in Aristotlean thought this focus on the human is reinforced by the belief that the distinguishing feature of persons was exclusive possession of rationality. These two tendencies taken together set the stage, over two thousand years ago, for the emergence of a civilization, our own, which countenances institutions that have entirely instrumental views of nature. Though it took centuries for this regrettable tendency to happen. The denaturalization (and desacralization) of nature found firm roots in the work of Descartes and Newton in the seventeenth and eighteenth centuries.

Darwin changes this: after his work the boundary or boundaries of morality have to be drawn differently, because the differences between us and the rest of nature become matters of degree only.

> The main conclusion here arrived at, and now held by many naturalists who are well competent to form a sound judgement is that man is descended from some less highly organized form. The grounds upon which this conclusion rests will never be shaken, for the close similarity between man and the lower animals in embryonic development, as well as in innumerable points of structure and constitution, both of high and of the most trifling importance, – the rudiments which he retains, and the abnormal reversions to which he is occasionally liable, – are facts which cannot be disputed.[9]

So treating equals equally can no longer be limited to persons. We can also see that Locke's self-preservation argument, joined to a rule of treating others as we would like to be treated – both developed in the previous chapter, must be extended beyond persons. The scope of morality can no longer be confined to persons.

Notice that this account easily covers and retains the core of human morality. It just moves the tent poles out. Actions that affect life have to be justified by reasons. We are no longer justified in acting as if nothing else is out there. There is no wasteland, no empty space. The obligation we already recognize among ourselves not to do gratuitous harm expands to include all of life. The right to self defense, which we recognize against other persons, is retained. The legitimacy of prophylactic behavior – vaccinations to avoid disease, steps to avoid water-bourne parasites, and other injuries – remains secure. Our concern is with the commonwealth of life: for its flourishing, including its own, and its restoration. Ironically, this line of reasoning may point the way to what is distinctive about us as humans: the ability to conceptualize and act upon these duties to all of creation; or, if you like, to the rest of life. But this difference does not set aside the duties.

Two factors are relevant in characterizing our duties to other forms of life. First, showing empirically whether or not there is a difference between human characteristics and the characteristics of other species. Second, if there is a difference, showing that it is morally relevant. Tall people are different than short people, but in most cases we don't think that the difference matters with respect to how they should be treated. Of course, in some cases it matters as when we determine who will be chosen for the basketball team, or who will be a jockey.

THE WIDENING CIRCLE

There are a number of candidates for defining the difference between humans and the rest of life: the ability to reason; to communicate through sound and signal; and to feel pain. None of these bounds the moral universe at persons. The ability to reason, communicate, and feel pain are found in numerous other species. These qualities, as Darwin pointed out over a century ago, are scattered throughout nature.

Let's start with pain. It is immediately evident that other animals with whom we closely share our lives feel pain in much the same way we do. Dogs, cats, and other pets, as well as farm animals like sheep, cows, and chickens evidently feel pain and react to it as we do; by crying out, by cringing, and by trying to avoid its source. Other animals more typically found 'in the wild' exhibit similar behaviors. The point that nonhuman animals feel pain hardly needs arguing.

Communication is also ubiquitous among human and nonhuman alike. Animals communicate about their pain. This communication brings assistance, relief from mental anguish, and warns others, and in some cases attracts predators. Animals communicate about their desires to mate, to nest, and about their need for food. Honey bees signal how to get to the presence of pollen sources – needed by the hive as raw material for making honey – by complex dances which can even describe the characteristics of the route to the pollen. Lions communicate with each other about the location of prey, beavers about the location of a leak in the dam, and dolphins about the location of mating partners. From an evolutionary perspective the ability to co-ordinate behaviors, through sound and signal alike, is highly adaptive.

So is consciousness generally. In *Animal Minds* Donald R. Griffin writes:

> The emergent property of consciousness confers an enormous advantage by allowing animals to select those actions that are most likely to get them what they want or ward off what they fear ... animals that think consciously can try out possible actions in their heads without the risk of actually performing them solely on a trial and error basis. Considering and then rejecting a possible action because one decides it is less promising than some alternative is far less risky than trying it out in the real world, where a mistake can be fatal.[10]

And the occurrence of consciousness is widespread, perhaps even a human-like consciousness:

[A]nimals are ... clearly more than mobile metabolisms. They appear to *act,* that is, to do things spontaneously, on their own. What they do is determined in large part by outside influences: yet the complexity and the remoteness of animal actions from whatever external causes may be what distinguishes them in an important fashion from microorganisms, plants, or physical systems. Most of these spontaneous activities are regulated by central nervous systems, and such systems, together with the adaptable behavior they make possible, are a special feature of living animals not found elsewhere in the known universe. In addition, members of at least one species also experience subjective feeling and conscious thoughts. We cannot be certain how common this additional feature actually is; but suggestive evidence ... makes it at least plausible that simple forms of conscious thinking may be quite widespread.[11]

Neither the ability to feel pain, nor to communicate, nor to reason survive as distinctive qualities of persons.

But perhaps there are other qualities that will allow us to continue drawing a sharp moral boundary between human and other animals. The ability to make contracts is often thought to be one of these. It is difficult to say whether or not other animals make contracts. In some species with lifetime mates, there may be something akin to a marriage contract – though we may never be able to know this. It is important, obviously, not to project our own values and frameworks on the rest of nature. It is equally important, however, not to assume that nature is a place without morality. Some species of animals clearly have expectations about each other's behavior from reproduction, feeding of young, sharing meat from prey, mutual protections and the like. There are contracts between persons and other animals as in the case of sheep dogs and shepherds, seeing-eyes dogs and their blind owners. Obviously, it would be better to know more than we do in deciding how to characterize our duties to other species.

At any rate the ability to contract is not the foundation of our moral obligations to begin with. No one doubts that we have obligations to protect small children, but it is clear that they do not have the ability to contract. It is their vulnerability – to feel pain, to be exploited by those more powerful than they are – that grounds our obligation to them. The empirical differences between adults and children are not decisive in this case.

The principles of self-preservation, equality, and stewardship extend naturally and inevitably beyond humanity. They are not limited to humans, but extend beyond humans, to the treatment of the rest of nature, insofar as we find the same characteristics beyond our own species. As Albert Schweitzer wrote in *Out of My Life and Thought*:

I am life which wills to live, in the midst of life which wills to live ... ,' As in my will to live there is ardent desire for further life and for the mysterious exaltation of the will to live which we call pleasure, while there is fear of destruction and of that mysterious depreciation of the will-to-live which we call pain: so too are these in the will-to-live around me, whether it can express itself to me, or remains dumb ... the man who has become a thinking being feels a compulsion to give every will-to-live the same reverence for life that he gives his own.[12]

We extend the golden rule to all within the commonwealth of life. We move, therefore, as Aldo Leopold suggests we should be in *A Sand County Almanac*, from a position of privilege in the natural world, to responsible member; from lord to steward. The progress project has now been turned on its head. It has gone from improving the human condition with nature as wholly instrumental to humans having special responsibility for fostering life generally.

There is no reasonable alternative to redrawing our moral boundaries to include all life. The will to live that I find in myself and my fellow humans I can find in some degree and in some manner spread throughout the living world. The basic elements of Locke's arguments remain intact: both the self-preservation part and the duty to treat as you would wish to be treated. To treat something differently than I wish to be treated I have to show that there is a difference between it and me, and that that difference is morally relevant to justify the different treatment. In the case of the principle of spatial equality – that everyone is entitled to equal treatment without respect to where they are – we saw that differential treatment was what had to be justified. A variety of reasons could count that justified this treatment. The same is true for citizenship within the commonwealth of life. It does not require that we treat a tree in the same way as we would a person, but that we justify why we are treating them differently. Reverence for life defines an outer boundary of obligation. Similarity or lack of it to humans defines the texture – the account of difference and corresponding duties – within that universe.[13]

HOW WE STAYED STUCK

We fundamentally misunderstand our place in the world due to reliance on an outmoded physical science which itself did not thoroughly question the anthropocentric inheritance of the western tradition. Our images of nature are multiple and include overtly religious and romantic notions. Yet, in our time there is a dominant image which has gradually assumed center stage since the seventeenth century. In constructing our public discourse we have inherited the *mechanics* of Newton. Newton's project was to find the same regularities in a terrestrial physics that Kepler had found in the smooth orbiting of the planets, and even to explain that orbiting. At the beginning of the *Principia* Newton stated that:

I derive from the celestial phenomena the forces of gravity with which bodies tend to the sun and the several planets. Then from these forces, by other propositions which are also mechanical, I deduce the motions of the planets, the comets, the moon, and the sea. I wish we could derive the rest of the phenomena of Nature by the same kind of reasoning from mechanical principles, for ... they may all depend on certain forces by which the particles of bodies ... are either mutually impelled toward one another, and cohere in regular figures, or are repelled and recede from one another.[14]

The idea is that the world is a machine that runs in one direction in a highly predictable fashion usually, or at least aspirationally, describable in mathematical terms. The elliptical orbits of large objects in space are taken to be guiding metaphors as we set ourselves the task of understanding the living world in which we move. As we will see in the next chapter this metaphor of the vast imperturbable machine underlies and lends legitimacy to the indifference of contemporary economics to its place within the nation of nature. It grounds the tragically misplaced confidence that we may massively intervene in natural systems such as climate and rivers with confidence that we can control the mechanically predictable results.

Contemporary ecological science tells a quite different story than that of imperturbable machine. Within the discipline of ecology, the breakdown of the Newtonian world view occurred in at least two stages. The first step was through the development of systems ecology, which sees the natural world as a set of interacting and evolving species, operating in niches that are themselves the result of long evolutionary processes, and that tend toward some equilibrium or climax. A forest will gradually evolve toward some equilibrium state, a wetland to some stasis that can endure until perturbed by exogenous event(s).[15] Much of the literature depicts events as a struggle, directly or indirectly for sunlight, in which the most successful organisms achieve a persisting dominance. The policy prescription thought to follow from this model is that of nondisturbance: to leave the equilibrium state as unperturbed as possible.[16] In this model the possibility of human disruption of nature comes front and center.

Critics of systems ecology argue that climax communities are at best rare. The norm is not stasis, but change. Like the ancient Greek philosopher Heraclitus they emphasize that the norm is change.[17] Look closely into what you think is a climax forest community and you will find change. Trees are blown over, afflicted with disease, attacked by parasites. Rabbits and other species affect which trees will reproduce successfully, and thus the future composition of the community. Nor does the idea of 'community' capture much of what is at stake. For though there is symbiosis in nature – organisms interacting in ways that benefit each of them – there is also competition, as each one struggles to capture the necessary energy for survival and reproduction. For the chaos ecologist, the question is not how can I keep or restore an equilibrium as it was for the systems ecologist; but rather in which direction do I wish to nudge the endless flux that I find around me, and of which I am a part.

Quantum physics moves us in the same direction. It describes a probabilistic world of energy fields, far from the perceptual constructs of everyday life. There is an interchange of energy and matter between objects that we often take to be separate and distinct. Water and microbes move between different objects beneath ordinary perception. The human self is a part of the field of flux. The me–it distinction erodes, the bifurcation between humans and nature collapses. We become identified with nature. Its state becomes our state, its health our health.

Nor are feelings only about the world, mere projections by us on to that dead and arid world of seventeenth-century epistemology. Quarks and joy are facts. The world is suffused with pain, ecstasy, lust, terror, anguish, and surprise. The frightened animal waiting to dart safely across the open space lives in us. We are that animal. The great divisions between life and matter only, between matter and spirit, between species, between persons, are marks on a continuum. They are of heuristic value in organizing thinking and directing action, but not rigid boundaries that are to be found in the world.

DUTIES TO ANIMALS WHO ARE NOT HUMANS

We have duties to respect the three basic rights of other persons including duties of mutual aid. This represents the moral minimum of what we owe other people. But what duties do we have to animals that are not persons? What are our nonanthropocentric duties? With regard to some of the other primates it seems reasonable to require that we should respect all three rights; with the exact duties depending on empirical descriptions. But it makes little sense to say that animals like chickens make moral choices, but then neither do senile people or babies. What we owe animals of this sort depends both on our relationship to the animal and to its characteristics.

ANIMALS IN OUR CONTROL

We owe animals in our care qualitatively similar duties to avoid unnecessary pain, stress, and to provide for their subsistence as we have toward members of our own species. Whether and how we can legitimately kill them for food depends on whether we believe they are capable of consciously valuing their own life and the manner of slaughter. The basic test is two fold. Insofar as they are like us we must treat them the same as we would a person. Insofar as they are different we may treat them differently, but we must describe the difference and fit the treatment to it. We don't owe rights of moral choice to animals that don't make moral choices, but we do owe avoidance of pain to those who can feel pain.

Clearly, the manner in which farm animals are treated in terms of confinement and force feeding need to be restricted if the animals show signs of stress, such as high levels of aggression toward each other. Thus the point of view argued here would require substantial revisions in trends in world agriculture, which tend more and more to mass handling of animals within an industrial model. The testing of cosmetics on animals would be ruled out on this model if it compromises their well-being, causes pain and the like.

ANIMALS IN THE WILD

There is no duty to rescue animals in the wild. Indeed, at least in the standard cases, there is an affirmative duty not to do so. This is so for at least three reasons. First, saving one animal will often simply imperil another. If we rescue the rabbit from the hawk we have just shifted the problem of survival from that of the rabbit to that of the hawk. Second, it would create godlike information and action burdens. We would have to pay attention to what is going on in the natural world in a manner that is not doable, and then take action to rescue one insect from another. This would create duties so comprehensive and onerous as to be incompatible with having a moral life of our own. Third, these rescues would raise havoc with the natural systems in which these animals reside since they would require massive interventions in ecological processes, and thus violate the duties to natural systems defended in the next section.

Is there a duty to refrain from killing animals in the wild? Are hunting and fishing wrong? Within the framework of the commonwealth of life the taking of a life must be justified by reasons. Deciding what to do within this overall framework requires looking at things empirically in considerable detail. Hunting and fishing simply for 'sport' do not justify the taking of the life of an animal that itself possesses the will to live. Eating and using the hide of an animal mitigate this effect, as life has not been lost simply for the purpose of entertaining the hunter. Still, the hunter must ask him- or herself the question posed by Thoreau: are the benefits achieved worth the cost in life to get them? It is important to note that this is *not* a move in the direction of conventional cost/benefit analysis where we sum up all the costs and benefits to affected persons and pursue those policies or actions that yield the highest net benefit. Rather we have to step outside of the anthropocentric ethic which cost/benefit techniques assume without argument and look at the action from a point of view which includes the cost to the animal hunted. If a overly large deer herd is destroying a forest through over grazing, hunting the deer may be justified, but we need to look at the question from a systems perspective not solely or even primarily in terms of the satisfactions of the hunter, or those who may dine on the venison.

The last large-scale hunting activity on the earth is commercial fishing. The decline of almost all the world's fisheries has resulted, in part, from using highly capitalized harvesting techniques within an industrial management model. One element, which we will discuss in the next chapter, was the idea that it did not matter if a fishery was ravished as long as the money made was invested in other resources yielding an equivalent or greater rate of return. This conceptual framework failed to focus both on the limited natural ability of the fisheries to rebound; and on the human social order that, in some cases, had lived in at least rough balance with the fishing stock. Within the framework of the commonwealth of life this is an unjustified taking for three reasons. First, these techniques unnecessarily damaged the ability of the stock to replenish itself by harvesting way beyond the regeneration rates. Second, in many cases these industrial techniques result in collateral losses to other species which can be avoided or substantially mitigated by, less intrusive harvesting methods. Third, the thinking that has led to the collapse of these fisheries also failed to respect the human traditions and ways of life that depended on the fishery for their well-being and survival. From the point of view of the framework that led to the present disaster just as the natural world is interchangeable with money, so are human institutions. In the impoverished world of neo-classical economics, if the men of Newfoundland can no longer be fishers let them move to Toronto and work in an office.

Nor is the rush to aquaculture (fish farming) the best path out of our mismanagement of the world fisheries. First, as presently practiced many of the issues of excessive confinement that occur with the raising of chickens and pigs occur here as well, at least with respect to certain species of fish. Second, this confinement often requires the heavy use of antibiotics to control the spread of infectious disease, and/or supposedly to stimulate growth. These practices often cause bacteria to grow that are resistant to the current generation of antibiotics. Having degraded the commons of the ocean we have now turned our considerable technical prowess to degrading the very 'wonder drugs' we have developed to protect ourselves. Third, aquaculture puts more pressure on land resources since it relies on the feeding of grain to fish. This, in turn, rests on intensive agricultural methods often harmful to aquifers due to the penetration of chemicals, topsoil loss, biodiversity reduction, and so on. If fish we must, it would be better to let the stocks in the ocean rebound to the degree they can than to rely increasingly on aquaculture. Of course, overall takes would have to be reduced. Sooner or later we will have to recognize that it is not the world fisheries that are too small, but the human population that is too large, especially with current consumption patterns.

DUTIES TO NATURAL SYSTEMS

Are there duties to ecosystems independent of the duties to the animals that reside within them? Within the commonwealth of life there are duties to plants not to take their lives gratuitously. If we wish our will to live to be respected so we must respect the will to live wherever we find it. But are there duties to the natural systems that we see around us: to wetlands, and forests? Within systems ecology, with the attendant ideas of systems equilibrium, community, climax, and the like, it made sense to talk about duties to restore or maintain balance. Systems had stable, emergent properties that were to be respected as such. It resonated with the image from Genesis of a completed world made by God.

The key issue is not stasis and change. Accepting the Heraclitean world of modern ecology and physics is not destructive of duties to nature. We can have duties to processes of which we are a part; to sanctify that from which we came.[18] The language of the contract tradition of which Locke is a part may appear to require that all duties are simply to other persons who are themselves capable of reciprocal promises. But we have already seen that for Locke not all obligations rest on promises; that the contract is a means of discharging antecedently given obligations. Natural-law obligations can express duties we have to the whole of which we are a part.[19] Within an evolutionary context we can have duties: to the process of evolution from which we have arisen and to which we now stand in a relationship of steward. Indeed, the structure of Locke's argument remains intact, though the object of concern is broadened from humanity to the commonwealth of life. The contract remains instrumental, a means to a broader end. And this is, of course, precisely the thrust of this book: the depiction of a contract between all persons to respect each other's basic rights, and to extend the contract to all of life.

CONTRASTS

There are a variety of schools of thought about the appropriate relation between persons and the rest of nature. First I will set them out and then consider how the fiduciary perspective relates to them.

FRAMING THE RELATIONSHIP BETWEEN HUMANS AND NATURE

Of the seven schools of thought I wish to summarize the first three are human-centered. The fourth is a method for thinking about the relationship between the present and the past. The fifth concerns the relationship between God or gods and nature, while the last two emphasize the continuity between humans and the rest of nature.

The Inherent Right to Take and Plunder

Historically this is the most important view, and it has certainly shaped our practices on both land and sea. This can be seen by the widespread transformations of the natural world over the past several centuries. It is often thought to be justified on biblical grounds that God gave humans the right to dominion over the earth.[20] The view that we may take what we wish from nature is customarily tied to the notion that all or most of the value of natural resources comes from the labor expended on them. This is a popular simplification of Locke's view. From this perspective, traditional nomadic or non-agrarian peoples establish little legitimate claim to land since they do little to improve property. This view also usually presupposes that resources are vast so that the taking on the part of one person does not diminish that available for others. In recent years a large literature has grown up in Judeo-Christian theology which argues in favor of stewardship of God's creation.[21] It shows, convincingly in my view, that the underlying Hebrew word translated by 'dominion' carries with it the notion of caring for.

Private Property and the Conservation of Nature

A related school of thought has grown up around the idea of private property rights.[22] Private property is alleged to be the best way to conserve resources because it avoids the 'tragedy of the commons': the tendency of people to reap the benefits of common property resources but not to care for them. Private-property owners have incentives to care for their property, to avoid hasty consumption in order to get a better price later, and to enjoy the benefits of liberty. In this school of thought it is argued that private-property owners will conserve those aspects of nature worth conserving. Typically it is argued that there is no standard independent of the desires of the owners of property to judge what should be conserved. Enclosure and other ways of establishing private-property rights are thus in the private *and* the public interest. This school also has a branch that emphasizes the duties of stewardship by private-property owners. These private stewardship duties were a major theme in some of Aldo Leopold's work in the 1930s and 1940s.[23]

Anthropocentric Utilitarian Arguments

Two other approaches to our relationship with the rest of nature find their roots in classical utilitarianism. Along with the first two schools listed, people who approach duties to nature through this lens assume that persons are properly dominant in the world (though as Bentham pointed out in the early 1800s the premises of the school don't support this since other animals also feel pain). Utilitarians hold that the fundamental principle of morality is the greatest happiness of the greatest number of persons.[24] Utilitarianism divides into two camps with regard to our attitude toward nature. In both cases resources are scarce.

The *bureaucratic utilitarian model* aims to assure an optimal resource flow into the future. This view is based on the ethical assumptions of classical utilitarianism, where assuring an adequate level of resources for future persons is emphasized. It is well developed in the writings of Gifford Pinchot, the founder of the United States Forest Service. Pinchot recast the fundamental utilitarian principle by adding that morality required that we seek the greatest happiness of the great number *for the longest time.* In this school of thought the present generation are trustees of a vast resource base that must be wisely managed, by government agencies, for the benefit of future persons. Pinchot explicitly rejected the idea of resource substitution with respect to forests, arguing that they were not simply the source of timber, but served to prevent erosion, to protect water supplies, and to provide places for wildlife and the aesthetic appreciation of nature.[25]

The *neo-classical market model* seeks to assure that the benefits of consumption exceed the cost. Its fundamental feature is the idea of maximizing human satisfaction through voluntary exchange. It has three essential elements.

1. Full-cost pricing, or *cost internalization* ensures that the goal of efficiency is met. The basic idea of internalization, as used by this school, is that the price of something as traded in the market should all include its costs up to the time that it reaches the consumer. (In some writings this idea is being extended to life-cycle costs – all costs through production, use, and disposal.) Suppose that producing tires causes air pollution, which damages someone else's laundry hanging out on the line. If we do not reflect the damage to the laundry in the price of the tires, society will produce too many tires. Thus the need to get the prices right. Markets are the solution once prices are properly set.

2. Discounting: While Pinchot explicitly rejected discounting and resource substitution this school of thought makes both ideas central. For a variety of reasons receiving money in the future is less valuable than receiving it now. If we had it now we could invest it. There is some risk that we won't receive it. People in the future are presumed likely to be richer than we are and hence, because of the declining marginal utility of money, it is likely to mean less to them. To make dollars that we receive at different times subject to a common

measure we need some way to treat them all as present dollars. Hence the dollars to be received in the future will be assigned a lower value than those received in the present, according to a formula that economists call the discount rate.

3. A third idea central to this school of thought is that of resource substitution. We typically do not need to worry much about running out of any particular resource because technology will find some way to substitute for it.[26] If we run out of copper we can make pipes out of plastic. Similarly, cinder blocks can be used instead of wood for building houses.

From the point of view of neo-classical economics environmental problems are economic and technical. We should get the prices right, including properly valuing the future through discounting, and invest in technological innovation for purposes of resource substitution.

Tradition Arguments

The role of traditions in framing environmental problems varies from culture to culture. In the case of the United States, Wallace Stegner argued, that the defining feature of American experience was the encounter with a continent that was primarily wild.[27] The constantly moving frontier to the west, the sense of vastness, the ability to begin again are what made us who we are. Once we have tamed all the wild places we will have tamed ourselves, and hence lost ourselves. A more generic version of this school of thought is contained in the work of Elinor Ostrom (see, for instance, *Governing the Commons*), who argues that traditional norms backed by a variety of formal and informal sanctions are essential for the preservation of common property resources. (We will return to Ostrom's work in Chapter 5.)

Religious Schools

There are a variety of versions of this point of view. God is *in* the world and to desecrate nature is to desecrate God (Muir). God is above the world, but nature is a necessary stepping stone to reaching God and enlightenment (Thoreau). God created the world and persons are the stewards of it (unfortunately only a minor theme in Judeo-Christian theology to date). This duty can be manifested as stewardship for the benefit of future persons or as stewardship of the biosphere. This kind of thinking about the relationship between humans and nature is not necessarily limited to monotheism. Many traditional cultures believe in a variety of gods who live in, or care for about, nature, or particular places in nature.

Extension School

The basic idea here is that moral duties extend beyond persons, and is the point of view defended in this chapter. Much of this line of thought comes out of Darwinism and argues that there is (1) no difference in kind between persons and other animals; or (2) what differences there are do not justify blanket differential treatment on the basis of species alone. There are also religious versions of this view sometimes found among traditional peoples. Many ecologists hold similar views.

Deep Ecology School

Deep ecologists make much of the commonplace observation that persons are intrinsically part of nature. They explicitly reject the dominion view which tends to dominate the first three schools. Modern lifestyles are grotesquely misleading and unhealthy, harming both ourselves and our planet. We have co-evolved with nature, and must keep this in mind in our lifestyles. This school denies that resources are necessarily scarce, emphasizing, in contrast, the beneficial effects of the moderation of desires. As we saw in Chapter 1 it is often associated religious views, similar to Buddhism, that the goal of life is the transcendence of the empirical self. We discharge our duties to nature by following nature's principle that nothing should be wasted: this leads to the principle of *materials* internalization. The modern 'development' process and resulting lifestyles are pathological from this perspective.

CHOOSING A FRAMEWORK FROM THE PERSPECTIVE OF THE COMMONWEALTH OF LIFE

How does the commonwealth of life relate to these schools? First, due to our commitment to equality of respect through time it will lead us to discard any theory that embraces universal discounting. Second, the fact of co-evolution with the rest of nature calls attention to the similarity between persons and other life, rather than to the differences that the doctrine of special creation highlights. This factor calls upon us to reject any philosophy of nature that is solely instrumental from a human perspective. Appealing to these two principles (of equality and co-evolution), let's re-examine our seven schools of thought. The inherent right to take and plunder can be tossed out because it explicitly treats nonhuman organisms wholly in instrumental terms, and because it at least implicitly allows discounting. Neo-classical economics explicitly allows discounting as a principle of planetary management, and also has an entirely instrumental view of nature. The bureaucratic utilitarian school cannot be what we are looking for, even though it rejects discounting and opposes large-scale resource substitution because it also sees nature in instrumental terms only.

The tradition school by itself is not what we seek because we have a variety of traditions, and we need some independent criteria for choosing which one or ones to emphasize. Neither can the private-property conception work taken by itself. The claims in favor of this school rest on the allegation that private property protects the resource base. But this is a contingent and empirical relationship depending on legal institutions that specify what private-property rights are, as well as whether or not the owners wish to conserve resources. So while the two branches of utilitarianism, market and bureaucratic, tradition, and private-property arguments could be *elements* in an adequate philosophy of nature, neither can serve as its foundation. So in considering various frameworks for thinking about the relations between humans and nature, this leaves us with the religious, the extension, and the deep-ecology conceptions.

The views of relationship between spirit and nature are probably as various as the logical possibilities. As we have seen, there could be a single god or a number of them. This God, or these gods, could be in nature, transcend it, have created and then abandoned it, have created it and still be acting in it, and so on. The views developed in this book are compatible with, but for reasons developed in this chapter, not dependent upon broad trends in Judeo-Christian-Islamic thought concerning the sanctity and goodness of Creation.

Deep ecologists take the next step. While extension theories point to the lack of difference between persons and other aspects of the natural world, deep ecologists point to the *common* features that we have with our co-evolvers. As discussed above, there is an identity between the human self, properly understood, and the natural world. To destroy it is to destroy ourselves. This is true both from the point of view of our material relation to the world since our bodies are in constant exchange with it; and in terms of our spiritual relations: the self that deep ecologist Arne Naess calls the transcendental Self. The commonwealth of life view differs from deep ecology in explicitly retaining human morality in the form of the three-way rights conception at its center.

THE CONSTRUCTION OF DIFFERENCE

The ideas of self-preservation, equality, stewardship, and the commonwealth of life have profound leveling effects on our thinking about the world. Traditional distinctions, some going back centuries or even longer, fade in the face of them. Nationality, group identity and responsibility, location in time and space, and even the species to which one belongs have been shown to take on a different character than one normally assumes. Reverence for life represents a moral bedrock that defines the foundation of morality. It takes us back to a beginning point, grounded in our own self-preservation from which to reconstruct the world.

The process of reconstruction will be both empirical and conceptual. The commonwealth of life does not obligate us to treat all plants and animals in the same way. It asks for a respect for all. It shifts the burden from the current anthropocentric conception of morality to a universal one. But it allows for differences based on appropriate understanding of other species, and the showing that those differences have moral standing. An understanding of what we owe the members of other species begins not in an account of our own sentiments, though our sentiments are by no means irrelevant as motivators to action, but is grounded in knowledge about what their lives are like. Do they feel pain? Do they reason? Do they experience fear?

Similar considerations apply to our obligations to persons. We have the universal duty to protect and enhance the basic rights of all. This obligation holds throughout both time and space. This defines a default morality toward other persons. But, of course, we do not owe all these obligations all the time. In many cases people's rights are adequately protected by themselves, their families, or their government. In the industrialized countries the bulk of the population has adequate subsistence. People who have relatively low incomes may have completely adequate food and housing. Many governments are very good at protecting the bodily integrity rights of their citizens.

The fiduciary conception of government set out in Chapter 4 argues for a series of defaults in securing subsistence rights. Individuals, families, communities are the first line. Trustee governments are second and discharge their duties both directly in securing these rights, and indirectly in fostering the institutions that support individuals, families, and communities. The international economy, other governments, and the emerging international civil society are the court of last resort for securing these rights. The shape of morality may be depicted as follows (see Figure 2.1).

Human moral concern spreads out from our location on the animal branch among the Eukaryota over all three domains of life. The default obligation is to treat all of life with respect. Beyond this requirement what we owe to the rest of life depends on two steps. First, on filling in the characteristics of the domains and their subordinate. Second, showing how these differences matter or fail to matter from a moral point of view. Of course, the diversity is many magnitudes more complex than this simple diagram, but it serves to represent the task ahead of us in constructing the morality of the commonwealth of life.

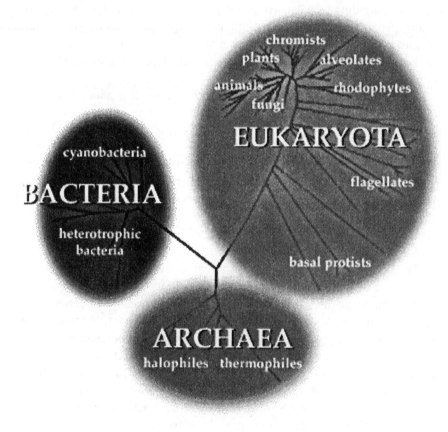

Figure 2.1 The three domains of life. The Bacteria lack a nucleus, the defining characteristic of the Eukaryota. The defining feature of Archaea is their ability to live without oxygen. (Reproduced with permission from the UC Museum of Paleontology.)

OBJECTIONS TO THE COMMONWEALTH OF LIFE

There are a number of objections to the commonwealth of life. First, it may seem a misuse of the idea of commonwealth itself. Caring for nonhumans may seem to be an expression of mere preferences or to be taken as a luxury good so as not to be comparable to the obligations of other citizens. Second, relocating ourselves as citizens within the commonwealth of life will be objected to as too vague, to lack specific guidance on what to do. Third, and conversely, it can also be taken to be too limiting – requiring that we treat all other life as sacred and untouchable. Fourth, it might be seen as too timid, of staying with a morality, or more accurately, a set of moralities that should be rejected altogether. Fifth, it could seem to rest on a romantic notion of nature itself; to underplay the tooth and claw elements of nature – even the tragic cruelty by which the weak are extinguished and the strong prevail.

IS LIFE A COMMONWEALTH?

Is the idea of commonwealth limited to a contractual, or contractual like, political community between different persons capable of deliberation and debate? Haven't I overextended a useful political framework? Clearly most of the elements of contracting do not apply between human and other animals, and the difference is even more radical, obviously, in the case of plants. But there are a number of ways in which this broadly democratic metaphor works. First, even within the human community we often speak on behalf of those humans who cannot speak for themselves. This is what we call the idea of substituted judgment, where one individual offers his or her judgment on what is best for another. For example, offering a judgment about what is best for a young child. Within the commonwealth of life this concept is simply extended beyond persons.

Second, the idea of the *common*wealth stresses the interdependence, and shared features, of the life forms that exist as a result of co-evolution. We are all in this together. Third, the common*wealth* dimension calls attention to the fact that we have an abundance to draw upon; that life creates a surplus. On earth, due to the constant influx of new energy from the sun, we live in a world in which increasing complexity is possible, and often the rule. Fourth, extending the conception of citizen makes clear the depth and scope of our resolve. Respect for the commonwealth of life is not a luxury good, to be indulged when we care to, to be ignored when more pressing matters are at hand. It is not something we do simply because it makes us better people when we do it;[28] though, of course, it does. It is, like citizenship in the customary case, a required profession of respect and the recognition of a common destiny – to which we pledge our sacred honor.

IS THE COMMONWEALTH OF LIFE TOO VAGUE?

Equality of persons, which I have argued above is a foundational principle of the progress project, requires that we treat all people with respect; a respect realized by securing their three basic rights. How this requirement is filled out depends on the characteristics and circumstances of the person. The grocer and the nurse are treated differently than each other, and differently in different circumstances. Nurses are treated differently when they themselves are sick.

The commonwealth of life is similar. It does not require that we treat all living things in the same way. It states a disposition toward the living world and then requires that how it is interpreted reflects the characteristics and circumstances of the organisms and systems with which we are involved. Much of the information we need to know is not fully available, in part because of the anthropocentric nature of much of current scientific research. In many cases we have merely assumed that other organisms do not think, or do not feel pain in the way we do without having fully investigated the question. The radical shift in framework occasioned by redefining our moral boundaries as the commonwealth of life is revolutionary, as was the ending – in many parts of the world – of human slavery. Vague it is not.

IS THE COMMONWEALTH OF LIFE TOO RESTRICTIVE?

As will become clear in subsequent chapters, accepting the commonwealth of life as the foundation of a philosophy of civilization requires very substantial revision of the status quo. Scientific research will be redirected, trade patterns changed, international law revised and enforced differently, farm and forestry practices revised, and the size of the human population reduced, to name just a few of the necessary changes. But the right of self-defense is retained, as is prophylactic behavior such as vaccination, medical research, and other means of promoting public health. The necessity of taking life to sustain it is recognized. We must walk gently on the earth, but we still must walk.

It might also be argued that the commonwealth of life is incompatible with political liberalism; and in particular with what might be taken as the rights of persons to treat other forms of life as they wish. In part, this charge cannot be avoided. Outlawing slavery certainly restricted the rights of former masters to treat certain people as they wished. But respect for the commonwealth of life is not at variance with political liberalism at its most fundamental level. For if political liberalism stands for anything at all it stands for the view that the good has a variety of forms. And respect for the rest of nature, for its variety and diversity, is then not in conflict with political liberalism, but may even be required by it.

IS THE COMMONWEALTH OF LIFE TOO TIMID?

It could be argued that more radical surgery is needed; that we need to reject a human-derived morality altogether. Perhaps making *human* self-preservation the starting point is just a form of narcissism reminiscent of what Schweitzer deplored decades ago. It could be argued that to avoid this we should repair to some standard of bio-equality; to seeing all life forms as of equal value. But this goes too far. Human morality is a complex set of rules and expectations. Were we to abandon it wholesale we would have little or no language with which to discuss what to do. It is the machinery that we have to work with now. Without it we would be completely at sea. What the conception defended here does is to open the door for the development and evolution of a broader morality now only in its nascent stages. Going to an alternative system such as bio-equality: the requirement to treat all life equally would be as absurd as a requirement to treat all humans equally independent of their differences.

IS THE COMMONWEALTH OF LIFE NAIVE SENTIMENTALITY?

One of the ideas at the heart of Darwinian biology and cosmology is competition. Much has been made of this feature of Darwin's thought, especially by Social Darwinists like Herbert Spencer.[29] Taking competition to be the fundamental law of nature, they attacked laws and conventions that protected the poor and the weak. In some ways free-market doctrines now in vogue are repeating these themes. But a more balanced view, and one shared by Darwin himself, is to see competition as *a* mechanism of nature along with other processes, including co-operation. Nature has no attitude toward individuals or the human species itself.

It is in our minds that the universe has become conscious of itself, though we do not know if we are unique. We can have an attitude toward beings other than ourselves. We can, and universally do, recognize duties to other persons who are not members of our own family, and hence are not close to us genetically. We seldom abandon competition altogether – witness the benefits of markets. But neither do we let competition rule the day unchecked. Antitrust laws that prohibit concentrations of economic power seek to restore the benefits of competition in the service of human progress. Laws prohibiting child labor rule out certain competitive practices. The commonwealth of life simply extends competition-enhancing, and competition-reducing, practices beyond our own species.

We now turn to the construction of institutions in service to the commonwealth of life.

NOTES

1. Personal note from series editor.
2. Richard Ashcraft, *Revolutionary Politics and Locke's Two Treatises of Government*, p. 266.
3. Psalm 115, Verse 16.
4. Peter Laslett, *The World We Have Lost*.
5. David Wasserman, 'Consumption, Appropriation and Stewardship,' in David A. Crocker and Toby Linden (eds), *The Ethics of Consumption: the good life, justice, and global stewardship*.
6. John Rawls, *A Theory of Justice*, p. 587.
7. See Steven C. Rockefeller and John C. Elder, *Spirit and Nature: Visions of Interdependence*.
8. Albert Schweitzer, *The Philosophy of Civilization*, p. 74.
9. Charles Darwin, *The Origin of Species and the Descent of Man*, p. 909.
10. Donald R. Griffin, *Animal Minds*, p. 260. Much of my argument that it is difficult to find a definitive boundary between humans and other animals draws on this volume.
11. Ibid., p. 254.
12. Albert Schweitzer, *Out of My Life and Thought*, pp. 186–8.
13. See, for example, Marian Stamp Dawkins, 'The Scientific Basis for Assessing Suffering in Animals' in Peter Singer (ed.), *In Defence of Animals*, pp. 27–40. An excellent compendium on the issue of the treatment of animals is Tom Regan and Peter Singer (eds), *Animal Rights and Human Obligations*.
14. Sir Isaac Newton, *Philosophiae naturalis principia mathematica*, 3rd edn, p. xviii.
15. See, for example, Eugene P. Odum, 'The Strategy of Ecosystem Development,' *Science*, vol. 164, April 1969, pp. 262–70.
16. See Alton Chase's *In a Dark Wood: The Fight over Forests and the Rising Tyranny of Ecology* for a discussion of the ways the idea that nature will find some equilibrium on its own can produce very undesirable results.
17. See, for example, Seth R. Reice, 'Nonequilibrium Determinants of Biological Community Structure,' *American Scientist*, vol. 82, September–October, 1994, pp. 424–35.
18. George Santayana, *Reason in Religion: Volume III of the Life of Reason or The Phases of Human Progress*. It is belatedly widely recognized that it is wrong to gratuitously trash the artifacts of human history such as the pyramids, the great cathedrals, the loci of famous battles, or the homes of famous, or in may cases, even infamous persons. It is not right to trash either the artifacts of human or natural history.
19. Mary Midgley, 'Duties Concerning Islands' in Robert Elliot and Arran Gare (eds), *Environmental Philosophy: A Collection of Readings*.
20. Lynn White, 'Historical Roots of our Ecological Crisis,' *Science*. 10 March 1967, pp. 1203–7
21. James A. Nash, *Loving Nature: Ecological Integrity and Christian Responsibility*.

22. Terry Lee Anderson and Donald R. Leal, *Free Market Environmentalism*.

23. Aldo Leopold, *A Sand County Almanac* and Susan L. Flader and J. Baird Callicott (eds), *The River of the Mother of God and Other Essays by Aldo Leopold*.

24. John Stuart Mill, *Utilitarianism*.

25. Gifford Pinchot, *The Training of a Forester*.

26. Julian L. Simon, *The Ultimate Resource*.

27. Wallace Stegner, *A Sense of Place*. See also Frederick Jackson Turner, 'The Frontier in American History.'

28. Immanuel Kant, 'Duties to Animals and Spirits' in *Lectures on Ethics*, trans. Louis Enfield, pp. 239–41.

29. Herbert Spencer, *Social Statics; or, The conditions essential to human happiness specified, and the first of them developed*.

PART II
FIDUCIARY
INSTITUTIONS

INTRODUCTION

Part Two argues that we need to re-envision economics, government, and civil society to exhibit their proper place within the commonwealth of life.

Chapter 3, 'Stewardship Economics,' argues in favor of a fundamental reconceptualization of economics, offering an alternative to the now dominant, even hegemonic, growth paradigm. The economics of stewardship builds on and extends the insight of John Maynard Keynes from the inter-war period that the goal of economics should be the prevention of war. Keynes's insight has become enshrined in current economic policy that seeks to preserve social stability through high levels of employment with stable prices. Stewardship economics carries this goal one step further – to the stability of the earth's life-support systems. The economy at the micro level, in the day-to-day transactions made by individuals, will necessarily be the result of individuals playing out their desires, interests, and convictions. At the macro level the economy must be limited by principles that respect the commonwealth of life.

Constructing an economics of stewardship involves answering a range of questions. What is the economy for? Where does and how should the economy fit in the physical and biological world of which it is a part? How much economic growth is enough? How should we think about the byproducts of the processes of economic production? How should we think about the future? And how can we generate the institutions necessary for markets to operate? This chapter shows how key terms in current mainstream – efficiency, internalization, substitution, marginality, protection, and cost – economics would be redefined within an economics of stewardship.

Chapter 4, 'Government as Trustee,' argues in favor of the idea of government as impartial trustee, an idea already deeply embedded in our thoughts and intuitions about government. Governments as trustees are answerable to the citizens to protect their basic rights, to conserve and use public resources wisely. It is an especially relevant conception of

59

government in which to ground public policy in an era that has witnessed the substantial degradation of the earth's resource base and the simplification of its biological systems. This chapter shows that the theory of market failures, the centerpiece of the neo-classical account of government and its legitimacy, is inadequate. The neo-classical model offers no account whatever of the role of the state in deciding where the market should operate, a fundamental obligation of all governments. It thus assumes away, without argument, a central dimension of the legitimate role of government.

Chapter 5, 'Civil Society in the Commonwealth of Life,' argues in favor of a three-way balance of power to protect and enhance the commonwealth of life. This balance involves government, the market, and civil society. All three groups of institutions need to be robust if we are to prevent the disastrous ricocheting between state and market that has characterized our era. Again, we are able to build on existing global trends in the arenas of human rights and the conservation of the biosphere.

This chapter highlights the characteristics of systems where humans have lived for long periods of time without degrading the natural resource base. The role of government and other ways of sanctioning resource-depleting behaviour are traced in controlling the behavior of rogues who would degrade natural systems. The nature of private-property rights and the duties that come with those rights are set out in the context of systems maintenance and enhancement. It is argued that the current transformative value conception of property rights, where we establish legitimate title to land and other resources by transforming them, must be replaced. We need to ground property rights in a new version of the ancient doctrine of the public trust, which recognizes our responsibilities to the commonwealth of life.

CHAPTER 3

STEWARDSHIP ECONOMICS

[T]he cost of a thing is the amount of ... life which is required to be exchanged for it.

(Thoreau, *Walden, or, Life in the Woods*)

The commonwealth of life requires a new economics. We begin by looking at current economics and definitions of its key terms. Then in the next section of the chapter six elements of stewardship economics, along with contrasts to the current regime, are set out. In conclusion stewardship economics is contrasted with sustainability and objections to it are considered.

CURRENT ECONOMICS

As we will discuss in Chapter 6 world economic integration has more and more gained center stage. It has become, and is becoming more so, the underlying theoretical perspective into which the rest must fit. Here we consider the building blocks of this framework both to examine economics in its more traditional national context, and to prepare the way to reconsider its international version set out and evaluated in Chapter 6.

The fundamental point of departure of this vision is the observation of the behavior of individuals who engage in exchange. This defines the domain of micro-economics. Each person who engages in a voluntary transaction with full information can reasonably be said to have benefited from the exchange simply because he or she did it. Or, in a slightly weaker version, he or she believed that the exchange would make him- or herself better off. The root idea is that of *consumer sovereignty*: the consumer knows his or her interests better than others and can act to advance them through exchange. Each consumer will pursue his or her opportunities until the *marginal* cost of a transaction exceeds the benefits of it. Thus each person maximizes his or her utility or happiness subject to the constraints of income by voluntary exchange.

This results in what is technically known as Pareto superiority, or a Pareto improvement, after the Italian economist Vilfredo Pareto. In such a transaction someone has been made better off without someone else being made worse off. In a Pareto superior transaction there is, by definition, net social benefit. But we can go beyond making things better. We can make them best. This is the frontier where there is no more space for improvement, where further transactions will result in someone being worse off. For example, if there are a fixed number of some desired goods any transaction making one person better off will mean making someone else worse off. This condition where improvement in overall utility is impossible is called Pareto optimality. It defines an *efficient* allocation of goods. The goal of policy from the point of view of micro-economics is to reach Pareto optimality, for here utility will be maximized.

There are complications, of course.[1] The two most important are externalities and public goods. The first, what economists call externalities, are factors in production or exchange where the price of a good does not reflect its true costs. More tires may be produced than is desirable if their prices do not reflect the air pollution associated with their manufacture. A key role for the public sector is to correct these prices by adding a tax (named after their proposer, Pigou) Pigovian taxes. These taxes recover the lost social cost of the externality. This is known as cost internalization and is a central feature of micro-analytical approaches to the environment.

Second, there are certain goods, what economists call 'public goods,' that don't respond to market signals. These goods are nonexcludable and/or nonrival. If we provide the good to someone we cannot avoid providing it to others, hence nonexcludability. If the Air Force protects me from nuclear attack it cannot help protecting my neighbor as well. Nonrival goods are those where exclusion may be technically possible, but where one person's consumption of the good does not detract from another person's enjoyment; for example, adding a few visitors to a large national park. In this way of looking at the world the task of the public sector is to remove, or at least to mitigate, the defects which are impediments on the road to maximum utility. This is the theory of market failures.

In this framework, the value of future events, the utility that we should attach to them, is assessed by calculating their value to us in the present. We need to have some way to compare an investment which will yield $1,000 in ten years to another that could yield $1,500 in twelve years. The way to make such a comparison is to calculate the *present value* of each. According to conventional economics there are a number of reasons for discounting. The present value of future resources is less than that of present resources, because if we had the resources now we could use them, so there is an opportunity cost for not having them now. If one investment is more risky than another we will have to assign it a discount rate. Or if we think future generations may be richer than we are, and hence have more utility, we may want to discount their well-being so as to avoid the poorer persons of the present generation from subsidizing the richer people in the future.

Another branch of economics takes its point of departure not from the behaviour of individuals, but from the study of the economy as a whole. Much of current macro-economics has its origins in the work of the English economist John Maynard Keynes. As he worked on *The General Theory of Employment, Interest, and Money* in the mid-1930s Keynes was worried that large-scale unemployment would lead to continued instability, especially on the European mainland, and to another world war. Furthermore Keynes realized that the utilitarian project of Bentham, Mill, and Sidgwick had (for reasons we will discuss below) run its course.[2] The general theory is thus a theory of macro-economics free of the utilitarian foundations which still underlies modern micro-economics. Keynes's project for the 1930s was a war-prevention strategy, but it came too late to head off the Second World War. The objective of the management of the economy for Keynes was not the satisfaction of desire as it is in micro-economics, but social stability. One of Keynes's principle arguments was that thrift in times of economic downturn is undesirable because it shifts resources away from consumption and thus causes unemployment.

During the First World War Britain had come perilously close to having to seek an accommodation with Germany for economic reasons. And probably would have done so if it hadn't been for American entry into the War. Working in the British treasury at the time Keynes believed that the British economy simply was not producing enough in goods and services to make it possible to finance the war effort. As the Second World War loomed a measure was developed, though not solely for this reason, that would rectify this difficulty, most particularly by American economist Simon Kuznets. This led to the development of a measure of total economic activity which was adopted by the United States early in the war. After the war it became a standard measure of economic performance. Hence the origin of the Gross National Product (GNP). This is a measure of all income received by residents of a nation for current services which are not transfers, such as payments to the elderly, plus appreciation in the value of stocks including, but not limited to, stocks in corporations, and then further adjusted for income received from abroad.[3] Gross Domestic Product (GDP) is the same as GNP except that the income from abroad is omitted.

The Great Depression was ended in Germany by Hitler's war-oriented stimulus package for Germany (Hitler was a Keynesian before Keynes!), and by the debt-financed responses to it by his military opponents in the Second World War. The surge in buying immediately following the end of the war was stimulated by savings accumulated during the war itself, and the downward edging of the US economy during the 1950s was delayed by the expenditures required by the Korean War. The revolutionary aspect of Keynes's approach was the intentional counter-cyclical stimulation of consumption to reduce unemployment. It provided the tools for the post-war boom in Europe and the United States once its basic tenets were accepted around 1962.[4] This has led us into the conundrum of having to stimulate consumption simply to keep the Keynesian squirrel cage from stalling, and the world from sliding toward instability and perhaps another catastrophic war. In the main Keynes's strategy has been successful. There has been no major conflict between the nations which adhered to his prescriptions.

As concern about large-scale war has diminished, attention has turned more and more to the proper management of the overall economy, and the desirability of removing any factors that could reduce overall efficiency as defined by micro-economics. Though many economists have been critical of Keynes in a variety of ways, including the tools for how to achieve growth, Keynes remains a strong influence in the background. The success of his theory legitimated the view that a primary job of government is to manage the economy to stimulate growth and to keep employment levels high.

Mainstream economics and stewardship economics may be seen as two edifices made of building stones.[5] In the process of this chapter I will show that current economics needs to be taken apart, but carefully. Many of the stones are essential elements in the needed reconstruction of economics within, not just atop, life's commonwealth. In stewardship economics many terms from the mainstream are repositioned and reshaped. These include 'objective function,' 'efficiency,' 'substitution,' 'marginality,' 'internalization,' 'protection,' and the nature of 'goods' themselves. I do not, therefore, reject the tools of economics, but only the current frameworks in which those tools are placed, and uses that are made of them in the current policy process. Indeed, many of my prescriptions for implementing a fiduciary agenda rely on reconceived and redirected macro-economic institutions and micro-economic incentives. I wish to replace the growth interpretation of macro-economics and the utility or welfarist interpretation of micro-economics.

STEWARDSHIP ECONOMICS

The elements of stewardship economics are set out in response to six questions: (1) What is an economy for? (2) Where does, and how should, an economy fit in the world's biophysical systems? (3) How much economic growth is enough? (4) How should we think about the byproducts of economic production? (5) How should we think about time? and (6) How can we generate the necessary institutions needed for markets to work correctly? The chapter concludes by contrasting stewardship economics with the idea of sustainability, and by considering objections to the fiduciary conception.

WHAT IS AN ECONOMY FOR?

What is the goal of the economy; what an economist would call its objective function? *The goal of stewardship economics is the restoration, protection, and enhancement of the commonwealth of life.* Mainstream economics has two goals that, at best, pull in opposite directions. Macro-economics aims to bring about high levels of employment with stable prices. It measures improvements in economic activity by increases in the Gross Domestic Product. Micro-economics aims at 'efficiency' to produce as much human well-being as possible through fair exchange.

The Purpose of Stewardship Economics

Stewardship economics respectfully alters Keynes's argument from the interwar period that the purpose of economics, the objective function we have about the economic system itself, is the protection of human life and culture.[6] As we have seen Keynes prudently pointed out the disruptive effects of large-scale unemployment in Europe, and its tendency to spark another war. Our aim should be similar, but broader, grounded in a concern for the commonwealth of life: the preservation and enhancement of the earth's life. Rather than construct a world view around the satisfaction of human desires we should begin with the whole system of which human life is a part, locate our species therein, and derive objectives from within the fiduciary conception. From this point of view the stimulation of overall demand, what Keynes called aggregate demand, the principle Keynesian tool for the creation of employment and hence social stability, must be evaluated from the perspective of its impact on life's commonwealth.

Implications for the idea of efficiency are revolutionary. The overall standard of efficiency in stewardship economics, what I call 'ultimate order efficiency,' is derived from this idea: that we treat all life with respect, and justify differential treatment. *Ultimate order efficiency* is what the economy itself aims for. In this framework the ultimate cost of a thing is how much life had to be exchanged for it, including but not limited to human life. Ultimate order efficiency sets the framework in which first order efficiency occurs – individuals and firms pursuing their economic interests, and the satisfaction of their desires, values, and interests. We can have efficiency within the economy, and we can have an idea of efficiency *about* the economy.

There are other kinds of efficiency. In *Beyond Growth* Herman Daly distinguishes four.[7] *Service efficiency* concerns the technical design of a product and the uses to which it is put in satisfying our desires. Some washing machines get our clothes as clean as others while using less electricity and soap. *Maintenance efficiency* is a measure of durability. Some washing machines last longer than others. *Growth efficiency* is the ability of ecosystems to replenish themselves as we take things we want from them. Some woodlots will keep me warm over multiple winters better than others, because they replenish themselves faster, or with wood yielding more BTUs (heat per cubic measure) or both. *Ecosystem service efficiency* is the measure of how much we disrupt the functions of ecosystems when we take things from them or dispose of pollution in them. How much erosion control, or wildlife habitat, is lost when I harvest my firewood? This efficiency is a measure of collateral damage. Each of these efficiencies define what we may call *stewardship policy space*. These are ways we can think about modifying and reducing our impact on life's commonwealth. We will return to this conception in Chapter 7 when we discuss the policy implications of the fiduciary model.

The Purposes of Stewardship Economics Contrasted with Those of Mainstream Economics

Mainstream economics in both its macro and micro forms offers an inadequate account of what the economy is for.

In the mainstream world the idea of progress has been compromised by being identified with economic growth as measured by the Gross Domestic or Gross National Product. These measures are sometimes referred to by the summary term: 'the national accounts.' From the point of view of the critiques offered here these measures are similarly troublesome. There are five reasons to abandon these measures: (1) GDP growth is a measure of activity, *not a measure of wealth*. Since accounts are not adjusted for declines in natural resources such as topsoil, oil, or forests, it is possible for aggregate income to go up and total wealth to decline at the same time. (2) GDP growth does not measure its own costs – much of what we spend may be to *defend* ourselves against unwanted side effects of GDP growth. If I buy an air conditioner to cool my bedroom made hot by urbanization GDP counts that as positive while it is really a cost. (3) GDP growth is *indifferent to distribution* of income and other goods generated by the economy – GDP can rise while poverty increases. (4) GDP growth is a *mismeasure of benefits* since it counts something that is bought and sold as a benefit while ignoring existing paid-for assets and things provided free such as housework or clean air. Indeed, the conversion of things that were free and later must be paid for counts as an increase in GDP while obviously we are not better off as a result. And (5) GDP growth takes no account of the *scale* of the economy relative to the biosphere on which it depends – how much of the biosphere is appropriated by the economy from other species, or how much it affects things like ecosystem and climate function. In general, it is important to see that GDP is an undifferentiated measure of benefits *and* costs. There is no way to tell if we are better off or not simply because we have more of it.

Looking for alternatives to GDP growth is not a denial of what most of the people in the world want: food, clean water, shelter, leisure, healthy children, and the like. The point is that GDP is an unacceptedly blunt instrument for figuring out whether these are being provided. It is ironic indeed that a measure adopted in the Second World War as means to determine war-fighting capability should become the prime measure of peacetime economic success. Despite its numerous defects it continues to be the main measure of 'progress' around the world. As we will see in Chapter 7 a much more disaggregated set of measures is needed.

Though GDP itself does not measure inequality, much of macro-economics is concerned with distribution. This can be seen in the emphasis on the creation of employment in the indicators used to measure economic performance. Job creation is a major tool that we have to reduce poverty, ensure subsistence rights, and improve economic well-being more generally. We must go beyond these tools. The only way unemployment can be addressed in this framework is by more and more aggregate growth. Obviously, this prescription is unworkable in a finite system unless we specify with considerable care, which the neo-classicists don't, what *kinds* of growth we are trying to promote. The destruction of ecosystems and the alteration of the world's climate itself are readily sacrificed on the twin altars of GDP and employment growth.

Let's turn to an examination of the objective function of micro-economics – efficiency: the idea that the goal of economics should be to produce as much happiness as possible. The following argument is not designed to prove that efficiency should never be a goal, but only that it should not be fundamental. A moral structure of society, of the sort argued for in this book, is required to set an order at what should be thought of as the constitutional level. This structure, once in place, will set the context for and constrain the idea of economic efficiency, not eliminate it.

The moral foundation of micro-economics is utilitarianism. This doctrine as formulated by John Stuart Mill in *Utilitarianism* 'holds that actions are right in proportion as they tend to promote happiness, wrong as they tend to produce the reverse of happiness.'[8] We should seek, according to utilitarians, the greatest happiness for the greatest number. In the philosophical literature written since the Second World War, there have been numerous serious criticisms of this doctrine. Micro-economics proceeds in the main as if this literature did not exist.

The utilitarian project has failed utterly to offer a satisfactory account of fundamental moral obligation for five reasons:

1. Utilitarians have been unable to show how to get from the (I believe false or untestable) proposition that everyone seeks to maximize his or her own utility, to the idea that we have a moral duty to maximize the utility of others, indeed everyone. As a moral system utilitarianism requires that we maximize the happiness of all affected persons. Yet it depends on the psychological premise that each person seeks to maximize his or her happiness. Absent heroic assumptions about interdependent utility functions (the degree to which one person's happiness depends on that of another) the premise that each person seeks to maximize his or her utility does not support the conclusion that we should maximize the utility of all.

2. In offering no place for the language of rights (Bentham referred to rights as 'nonsense, nonsense on stilts'[9]), classical utilitarianism authorizes the ruthless exploitation of a minority if a net gain in utility can be projected. Numerous attempts to rescue utilitarianism from this defect by arguing that we can reconstruct the language of rights out of summary rules are unsuccessful. This is because in each case we still have to decide whether *this* action that I am considering will lead to the maximization of utility even if it means overriding the rule.[10] Rule utilitarianism always collapses back into act utilitarianism.

3. Utilitarianism is infeasible from a motivational point of view in the classical version (greatest happiness of the greatest number) because it requires more altruism than we can reasonably expect people to muster. In calculating what to do I must count my own happiness as only one in perhaps a very large group; say given the world's present population one in six billion. Further, it is impossible to maximize two variables: do we seek more happiness or to spread it over more people? The self-interested motivational assumption of the neo-classical school fails for the opposite reason in that it fails to offer any account whatsoever of what we owe one another.

4. As an examination of its texts reveals that some of modern economics tries to distance itself from the failures of utilitarianism by dropping the language of utility in favor of that of preferences or tastes. It would appear that since they are not talking about utility then they can escape being entangled in the defect of utilitarianism. This strategy backfires. If preferences and tastes are not connected to utility then it is completely mysterious why one should care about them; or about why one should care about the satisfaction of other people's preferences.

5. A utilitarian should consider the preferences of at least some nonhuman animals since many of them can also experience pleasure and pain, and they surely also have preferences and tastes. Worms reveal their preferences for sidewalks as contrasted with lawns after rains by crawling on them. Since this is a preference why shouldn't we be concerned with satisfying it?

Macro and Micro

It is important to see that the objectives of efficiency and GDP maximization are unlikely to coincide. This is so for a number of reasons. The first has to do with the failure to distinguish between activity and wealth. For example, clear cutting forests on steep slopes may raise GDP in the present while depleting wealth, and also causing widespread, long-term, and uncompensated ecological and social havoc. Therefore utility is not maximized. Second, GDP growth can be uneconomic when seen from the perspective of efficiency. It can cost us more to defend ourselves against the side effects of economic growth than the benefits conferred by the growth itself. Third, we may often get more GDP growth by not internalizing costs, than by internalizing them. If we raise the costs of tires, consumers will buy fewer of them. If we let tire producers dirty Mr Jones's laundry we will get more tires consumed because the price of tires will be lower – expanding GDP, and Mr Jones will have to do his wash more often – also expanding GDP.

Thus the objective functions of current macro- and micro-economics taken singly, and taken together, fail.

WHERE DOES, AND HOW SHOULD, THE ECONOMY FIT IN THE WORLD'S BIOPHYSICAL SYSTEMS?

Stewardship economics explicitly sees the economy as imbedded in the earth's biophysical systems, and framed by norms cognizant of the commonwealth of life. Mainstream economics offers no account of its location in the physical world, and offers no fundamental norms other than the expansion of Gross Domestic Product and the stimulation of employment in the case of macro, and efficiency, in the case of micro.

Stewardship Economics and the Commonwealth of Life

Keynes entitled his work on the restructuring of economics *The GENERAL Theory of Employment, Interest, and Money*. I have emphasized the word 'general' because Keynes is saying that the old economics, for example, that of Says – who held that supply creates its own demand – is not wrong, but it is a special case. Like Einstein's theory of special relativity, which holds under limited circumstances, Keynes is saying the same thing about economics up to his day: it is a special case. Keynes saw his theory, not quite rightly, as *general.* It broadened the institutional context of the economy to include an active role for government in the stimulation of economic activity in times of recession and depression. But like the special theories it sought to supplant, Keynes theory still ignored the broader context of human economics.

Stewardship economics extends, and may hope to complete, the quest for a general theory by explicitly locating the human economy in the earth's biophysical systems. It requires therefore both an accurate description of the economy in those systems and a normative structure that will allow us to say how these systems should function.

Stewardship economics recognizes the finitude of the earth and its systems. We need to begin with descriptions of these systems. We might begin with water, energy, and materials balances. Some examples are given below. Obviously, complete descriptions will be much more complex.

1. Water: there is only so much water on the earth. There is no way to change the total amount of water available to life, and the ratios between salt and fresh water cannot be altered to a significant degree given current technologies. Obviously, it is not the total amount of water that is mainly at issue, but where it is, its physical state (ice or vapor), and its ability to support life directly as habitat and indirectly through commerce. Many of the issues central to life's commonwealth will have to be resolved on a watershed-by-watershed basis.

2. Energy: we also have to be concerned with the characteristics, amounts, and consequences of using our energy supplies. The amount of energy reaching the earth during the life of the sun is fixed. Most of it is radiated back out into space, small amounts have been stored in coal, oil, and natural gas, and in the biosphere. These represent the stock of resources available to us. How fast we draw down these stocks represents one element of the flow of energy – of stored sunlight. The other element of the flow is how the sunlight reaching the earth each day is used. This is basically a question of the extent and characteristics of photosynthesis, technical means of capturing the energy of sunlight such as photovoltaic cells, and to a lesser degree the use of wind power. Other energy sources such as geothermal, tides, and nuclear are relatively minor in their ability to contribute to overall energy demands. Re-evaluation of expanded reliance on nuclear sources may be justified in conjunction with vigorous conservation efforts – currently marginal efforts at best in some of the richer countries.

   Again, much of our attention will have to be paid to particulars. What is the impact of various energy strategies on the ability of human communities to protect basic rights and on the ability of other species to flourish? For example, the burning of biomass – such as residues from logging and farming – for the production of electricity may reduce soil fertility and species complexity. Heavy reliance on fossil fuels is substantially altering the earth's climate and imperiling the habitat and even the continued existence of many species through changing the zones in which plants and animals can live, altering water temperatures and depths, changing the patterns of monsoon rainfall, and eradicating coastal wetlands.

3. Materials Balances: the earth's temperature balance is determined by the interaction of the energy from the sun and the characteristics of the earth's surface and the gases that compose its atmosphere. At this time more carbon dioxide is introduced into the atmosphere than is taken out. It is virtually certain that this is causing a rise in the average temperature of the earth. A partial list of the magnitudes of some of the earth's systems is contained in the Appendix at the end of this book, along with estimates of the degree of human perturbations of those systems by a number of elements including heavy metals and a variety of nutrients. The effects of these imbalances on life's commonwealth have to be estimated to allow an assessment of their impacts.

The norms that should govern the relation of economics to the physical world are first the obligation to provide for the three basic rights, most particularly subsistence and second the obligation to respect the flourishing of other species. The first obligation will tell us the amount of farmland we need relative to any given technology, climate, and consumption patterns. The second will constrain the use of some resources in ways already discussed under efficiency. The prolific use of water in the western United States for golf courses and fountains in the desert, resulting in the extirpation of some species, is clearly a disallowed use within the framework of the commonwealth of life.

Mainstream Economics and the Biophysical World
Perhaps the most astonishing fact about current economics is that it provides no account of where the economy *is*. In standard economic textbooks the economy is depicted in Figure 3.1. The fact that the economy is in the world, in its physical and biological systems, is simply not recognized by this model. There are a number of reasons to regret this. First, it legitimates on an outmoded model of the way the world works. Second, it has tragic implications for the rest of nature, which is seen as made up of interchangeable parts. Third, it leads to a misunderstanding of resource abundance and scarcity.

Perhaps the most pervasive scientific error made by mainstream economics is that it carries forward, as an unexamined background assumption that humans are not significant actors in the earth's biophysical systems. In most economic texts there is no description of any kind of nature. There are often few, if any, entries under environment, natural resources, nature or other cognate ideas. It is as if the rest of the physical world did not exist or that humans could not affect it. But, at the very commonsense level we know that this picture is completely misleading. Humans are instruments of change from the micro-environment to the global level, from what goes on in our own blood streams to the shape of mountains and the course of rivers.

Figure 3.1 The Circular Flow Model
The circular-flow-of-income model illustrates that economic activity is circular. The inner circle shows the flows of physical goods and services and of inputs through the system. Firms supply goods and services that are demanded by households; households supply inputs that are demanded by businesses. The outer circle shows the flows of money. Households spend money on goods and services that flow to businesses as revenues; these revenues flow to households as payments for supplying their inputs.

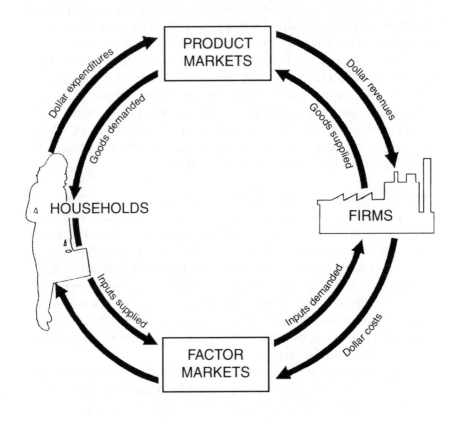

Source: Katz, M. and Rozen, H., *Microeconomics*, 3rd edition (McGraw Hill, New York, 1998), p. 9, diagram 1.2.

The world is made up of complex adaptive systems. It is not the Newtonian world, where for every action there is an equal and opposite reaction, but a world in which complex adaptive systems respond in ways that are difficult to predict. Once an equilibrium is perturbed we cannot predict with assurance what the new equilibrium will be or whether it will be desirable. Even though economists have often described the complex, multi-faceted aspects of human behavior with great sophistication, these insights are not carried over into their views about nature.

Mainstream economists typically assert that we need to have economic growth so that we can then be rich enough to afford the cost of cleaning up environmental problems. The argument is that as wealth rises people's preferences for environmental goods will rise as well.[11] There are at least two problems with this idea. First, it presupposes that economic growth is making us richer – thus begging the question at issue as to whether or not growth at the margin is *un*economic. Second, the notion that we can mess up nature and then clean it up implies that nature is like an industrial process where we can make any artifact that we want. This is not true. First, natural processes are not reversible as this assertion implies: species loss and carbon-dioxide loading of the atmosphere which leads to climate change cannot be repaired by any amount of money within historic time periods. Second, natural processes are capable of exponential, not just linear, change as the mainstream model supposes. Ecosystems sometimes respond gradually to change and then suddenly flip to a new level of organization.[12] Third, nor does this view address what happens to the well-being of those injured – human and nonhuman alike – by polluted air and water while wealth is allegedly rising. Fourth, the rising incomes scenario implies that all environmental damage is local, so that people can clean up the mess that they have made in their own backyard. But environmental problems like global warming are not confined to the countries that generate them.

There are *some* types of economic change that improve *some* environmental conditions such as more efficient cars that pollute less and thus help reduce air pollution in metropolitan areas. But much economic growth contributes to environmental deterioration. Housing developments that are built in the countryside depend on septic systems that pollute the groundwater, require extensive road systems that alter runoff patterns, destroy habitat, are visually disruptive and last – at least in terms of historic time – indefinitely.

Moreover, the neo-classical view fails to take into account the great difficulty in knowing whether the environment is declining or not. Each person who is born sees the world anew and takes as the benchmark the world as he or she finds it. This point of departure serves as at least an intuitive guide as to whether things are improving or not. As a result detecting long-term historical trends is difficult for the 'man in the street.' Here is how Farley Mowat in *Sea of Slaughter* contrasts the world of the western north Atlantic today to that found by early European explorers and exploiters:

> The living world is dying in our time.
>
> I look out over the unquiet waters of the bay, south to the convergence of sea and sky beyond which the North Atlantic heaves against the eastern seaboard of the Continent.
>
> And in my mind's eye, I see it as it was. Pod after spouting pod of whales, the great ones together with the lesser kinds, surge through the waters everywhere a-ripple with the living tides of fishes. Wheeling multitudes of gannets, kittiwakes, and other such becloud the sky. The stony finger marking the end of the long beach below me is clustered with resting seals. The beach itself flickers with a restless drift of shorebirds. In the bight of the bay, whose bottom is a metropolis of clams, mussels, and lobsters, a concourse of massive heads emerges amongst floating islands of eider ducks. Scimitar tusks gleam like a lambent flame ... the vision fails.
>
> And I behold the world as it is now. In all that vast expanse of sky and sea and fringing land, one gull soars in lonely flight – one drifting mote of life upon an enormous, almost empty stage.[13]

Those of us who experience nature now are witnessing, in many cases, a mere remnant of the natural world as it once was. But only those who have taken the trouble to understand natural history know this. Most economics departments do not even teach the history of their own discipline. Even here, their focus on the margin, on the next change, keeps them from seeing, or even seeking, the whole picture. They are content with sub-optimization – making the best of an ever-worsening situation.

Some economists, typically the school of thought known as technological optimists, point to the fact that real prices (prices adjusted for inflation or deflation) are falling for most of the inputs to industrial society,[14] and if shortages should occur we will be able to substitute for them. There are two arguments here: one about prices and the other about substitution, both problematic.

1. Prices and Costs: the claim about real prices normally doesn't even pass the test set by neo-classical economics itself. To do this it would have to take into account all of the side effects of production, use, and disposal of goods. But this is not done. The fall in 'real' prices of many natural resources is less real than it seems because extraction and processing of resources involve costs that are not reflected in the prices, these costs are what economists call 'externalities.' For example, much of the 'industrial forest' of Northern New England and the Canadian Maritimes is sprayed with chemicals to inhibit the growth of hardwoods. These chemicals have ubiquitous and difficult to trace effects on wildlife, including commercial and sport fisheries, which are not reflected in the costs of pulp wood, and inhibiting hardwood growth changes

the price of flooring and baseball bats. Similar points can be made for many other inputs of industrial society.

In addition, there are limits to the biosphere's ability to absorb waste, and these limits are already being exceeded, both locally and globally. In the United States the Chesapeake Bay, once one of the world's most prolific fisheries, has undergone a substantial collapse, due in large part to polluted runoff from suburban development and agriculture, as well as overfishing and the introduction of exotic organisms. At the global level, the ability of the atmosphere to recycle carbon into the earth's crust is vastly exceeded, very likely resulting in accelerating climate change.

Nor do low prices by themselves necessarily signal resource abundance, even ignoring failure to achieve full-cost pricing. Producers of natural and other resources can be trapped into price-cutting actions simply because they have no other options but to sell at world prices. For example, it is likely that many of the world's tropical forests are being liquidated at foolishly low prices because the countries in question have no quicker way to earn the foreign exchange necessary to participate in a globalized trading regime. The low price of a good may not signal abundance, but production at prices set by desperation.

Both the technological optimist and the more sober neo-classical economist have failed to answer the question: costs to whom? From the fiduciary point of view the idea of costs needs to be expanded. The food we eat not only cost us money and the time, efforts, and sacrifice it took to earn it; it cost the world's ecosystems something to produce. It used part of the earth's finite energy supply. If the good is meat its production cost the animal its life, and probably some suffering. Those who sacrifice little for their money may tend to think that the world sacrificed little for what they buy with it. Even if price distortions are corrected according to neo-classical prescriptions, the moral problem of fulfilling our stewardship duties is not.

2. Substitution: nor is the substitution argument as simple as it appears. These arguments work mainly by construing the use of resource in very narrow consumption terms. For example, from a *resource* point of view the collapse of the north Atlantic cod and other ground fisheries is not a matter for much alarm because soybeans or other proteins such as chicken can be substituted in human diets to replace that no longer available from the fish. Taken in these terms the argument carries the day in the main.

But there is no reason to take it on these terms alone. The amazingly complete commercial destruction of this resource does not simply give rise to a crisis of protein. It has deleterious effects on employment, the economic core of the region, and a way of life for humans stretching back to nearly to the year 1500 for Europeans and even earlier for the traditional peoples whom the Europeans displaced. But seeing this, which the neo-classicist does not, is to see only a portion of the ensuing disaster. The removal of several kinds of fish from a great fishery can be a catastrophe for the remnant bird, seal and other species who must also make their livelihood from this source. A common result is the starvation of the young. What appears to be a factual claim on the part of the neo-classicist gains its plausibility from an account of the person-as-consumer and of the responsibility of persons toward nature that are both completely inadequate.

The trusteeship framework gives us a different perspective on substitution. Gifford Pinchot argued nearly a century ago in *The Training of a Forester* that forests serve a broad and irreplaceable cluster of functions in addition to their role as sources of raw material: erosion control that protects streams, bays, and lagoons; the cleansing of water for use by humans and wildlife; the mitigation of heavy runoff, which would otherwise cause floods; a home for wildlife; a source of recreation; a source of aesthetic contemplation, and so on. Viewed with their broad functions in mind, forests are not technically or morally substitutable.

The very idea of substitutability is recast within an ethics of stewardship. A steward seeks the preservation and, where appropriate, the restoration of persons and the natural world. This sets the standard by which we assess the desirability of substitution, following the structure of the fiduciary duties. Advances in agriculture which allow for the conservation of topsoil and/or the restoration of excess and/or abused farmland to woodland and wildlife habitat are desirable substitutions. Stewardship of climate would serve as a major catalyst for technological innovation since dramatic drops in greenhouse gases would be required. Tax increases to reduce emissions, and tax incentives for new technologies and other ways of spurring reductions in greenhouse gases will have to be centerpieces of the stewardship of climate. There would be robust substitution within stewardship economics, but its composition would be different, and it would be in service of different goals than in the current framework. We may state a principle that parallels Leopold's statement of the land ethic:[15] substitution is good when it tends toward the conservation and restoration of persons and natural systems, bad when it tends otherwise.

HOW MUCH ECONOMIC GROWTH IS ENOUGH?

From the fiduciary perspective the economy should steer a course between being insufficient to supply the goods necessary to protect basic rights – most particularly subsistence rights – and not so large as to compromise the ability of other species to flourish. Mainstream economics has no answer to the question of whether the benefits of economic growth exceed its costs, and no way of calculating the appropriate size of economic activity relative to the biosphere on which it depends.

The Scale of Stewardship Economics

Though many people in the world do not have their subsistence rights guaranteed, the *aggregate* amount of food and other necessities for this purpose is more than adequate. Of course, tragic abuses of subsistence and other basic rights occur in many countries for a combination of institutional, economic, organizational, and environmental reasons. One of the purposes of this book is to show that national borders are not the ultimate determinants for deciding who has the obligation to secure these rights; that these obligations default to the international community. We are over the necessary threshold on the low side, but need considerable institutional reform to meet our obligations to secure basic rights on a day-to-day basis. In a world arranged according to the principles of transparent sovereignty within the commonwealth of life, systematic starvation and malnutrition would be unknown. Of course, the best way to secure these rights is most likely to be local institutions accountable to the people whose rights are involved.

On the other side of the permissible range, chaos reigns. The current mix of population size, consumption patterns, technology, and an economics indifferent to the well-being of nature are bringing havoc to many natural, not to mention many human, communities. According to stewardship economics, as we will see, certain ecosystems could be set partly or largely off limits to human use; and others could be managed in manners that do reduce their ability to regenerate after use. *The space between the lower boundary of satisfying basic rights, and the upper boundary allowing other life forms to flourish, is the space for legitimate human wealth.*

The Scale of Mainstream Macro-economics

The principle of marginality which is central to micro-economics says that we should stop any activity when its costs exceed its benefits. We continue an activity up to, but not beyond, the point when the benefits exceed the costs. We do what is most important to us first, then what is second, third, and so on. We spend our last dollar on what we value least. This way we can satisfy our most central desires the most. While there are numerous reasons we will explore why this should not be a fundamental principle of choice, it does offer a means of deciding how much of something we want. Macro-economics offers no comparable principle, no way to tell when growth has become uneconomic.

Even from a conventional anthropocentric view of the world we should use the resources that matter the least in terms of ecosystem function first, then the next valuable, and so on. But this is not what we do. Wetlands of enormous ecological importance are routinely destroyed. Prime farmland is carelessly committed to urban uses without significant, nay, in most cases *any* thought to other ways of accomplishing the objectives in question. Once we see an obligation to respect the commonwealth of life, the lack of a principle of ecosystem marginality, of what to use first, what last, later, or never, becomes even more evident, even more painful to witness.

The fiduciary perspective helps to redefine the idea of marginality. It reframes cost/benefit analysis by broadening the concept of both costs and benefits. The question of marginality from the point of view of stewardship economics is two fold. On one side, will the change in question move us away from or toward the protection of the three basic rights? On the other, will it move us away from or toward respect for the commonwealth of life?

HOW SHOULD WE THINK ABOUT THE BYPRODUCTS OF ECONOMIC PRODUCTION?

By what standards should we judge the processes of production that serve the economy? *From the point of view of stewardship economics industrial processes have to be analyzed with a view to their effects on the whole commonwealth of life.* From the mainstream perspective any industrial process is permitted so long as the costs as reflected in the market are fully internalized.

Production in the Stewardship Model

Stewardship economics requires the reconceptualization of industrial processes and waste.

Once we see the nested limits of the world in which we live we can recognize that we are pushed in the direction of materials internalization, not price. Karl Henrick Robert and his colleagues in the Natural Step Movement in Sweden have formulated the basic principles involved, and I discuss them here.[16]

1. Materials from the earth's crust, the lithosphere, should not be allowed to accumulate systematically in the ecosphere. Heavy metals like lead and cadmium are good examples of materials that we should keep out of the realm in which life exists. The goal is not that the person who wants to use lead in a battery should pay all the costs of that use, but that the lead should be managed with the goal of preventing its release into the biosphere to begin with. These substances have a life cycle from mining to disposal. Within the fiduciary system the goal is the control of that substance throughout that cycle to avoid dispersion during the period of use. There is no need to estimate a substance-by-substance damage function.

   Some materials from the earth's crust have a natural cycle. It is not their release into the biosphere that is crucial, it is their balance. Carbon is a good example, though, of course, a certain amount of carbon is necessary for life at all. Carbon is removed from the atmosphere by being taken up in either terrestrial or aquatic plants. If these remain in the biosphere the storage is relatively temporary lasting only until the organism decomposes. If the organism sinks to the ocean floor, particularly if it covered by other sediments and moved into the earth's crust by plate tectonics the removal is very long term. From the point of view of materials internalization the goal is cycle balance: emissions into and extractions from the atmosphere should be in rough equilibrium. Of course, price changes may be a means to move us in this direction.

2. Materials from society should not accumulate systematically in the biosphere. In addition to the issue of naturally occurring substances such as carbon that can get out of balance there are tens of thousands of compounds that have been made by humans that are accumulating in the biosphere. This is in part attributable to current macro-economics. Since markets for many existing products are satiated, stimulating further consumption requires novelty to inspire consumers to buy the new item. Product innovation depends, in many sectors, on chemical engineering that introduces novel and typically untested substances into the environment. For example, there is considerable evidence that a variety of substances that disrupt human (and other organisms') central nervous, immune, and reproductive systems are widespread, perhaps even ubiquitous in the biosphere. These effects are sometimes irreversible for the individuals affected, as in the case of persons who are rendered sterile due to the effects of chemicals during their embryonic development. In addition, as manmade compounds move up the food chain they often become bioconcentrated as organisms consume one another. For example, high levels of industrial chemicals are precipitated in the arctic because of temperature and wind patterns. They are concentrating in the food chain of humans and other species. From the point of view of stewardship of the commonwealth of life these tendencies should be resisted. The burden of proof for the introduction of new substances should be on those who want to introduce them. They should have to show that their impact on life's commonwealth is benign.

The idea of waste is reconceptualized within the fiduciary framework. In the neo-classical view, waste causes unnecessarily unsatisfied human desires. The buck who dies of old age in the forest is a wasted deer, having frustrated the hunter's desire to bring him to ground with a bullet. In the fiduciary conception waste is life unnecessarily foregone. For this reason the resources of the biosphere should be retained within it. In the western industrialized countries sewage is regarded as something to be gotten rid of. Indeed, one of the most, perhaps *the* most, substantial advance in human health was brought about by keeping sewage segregated from water supplies. There can be no quarreling with this outcome.

The fiduciary perspective sheds a different light on how we should think about sewage. It is not truly 'waste', but an asset out of place. Sewage contains the results of photosynthesis. It represents an investment of the earth's limited capacity for the production and sustenance of life. Sequestering it from the biosphere by burying it in land fills, or burning it, represents a waste of the earth's capacity to support life. Similar considerations apply to garbage generally.

Byproducts within the Neo-classical Model

A central feature of the neo-classical model is the idea of correcting prices to reflect all costs associated with production, consumption, and disposal of goods. While stewardship economics will, as we will see, rely on prices as a means to preserve and protect the commonwealth of life, it does not seek an optimal efficiency as defined within the framework of consumer sovereignty. Seen from the fiduciary perspective there are a number of problems with the corrected prices mantra.

The price-internalization model fails to take into account the difference between a harm and a wrong. It is wrong to do some things even when we compensate for them. It is wrong to rape someone even if you pay her or him later. Yet the idea of corrected prices just says we should pay for the harm that we do. The cognate idea that the 'polluter should pay' has the same defect when used without relation to principles designed to answer the question: pays for what?

What in fact happens in setting public policy is that a set of factors exogenous to the market determines which externalities we try to control. For example, many environmental laws having to do with clean air and clean water, as we have seen, draw their moral authority from concern for the vulnerable, not the idea of cost internalization. In some cases we can move toward protecting the vulnerable by internalizing costs, but in most cases the efficient level of pollution will leave those most susceptible to pollution inadequately protected. Suppose the number of people with impaired lung capacity is 10 per cent of the population. Damage to their lungs is unlikely to weigh heavily in arriving at an overall assessment of net costs and benefits. Hence they are likely to be placed at risk by this decision rule, and this is considered to be wrong.

For the price-internalization model to work we must be able to estimate the value of the damage in question to know how much to correct a price. Take the case of climate change. How much damage climate change will do in India a hundred years from now is a question to which it is not possible to develop a reliable answer. We don't know what the technology, agriculture, or settlement patterns will be at that time. Yet each of these will be significant factors in projecting the impacts of climate change. Nor do we know how to calculate the costs of the damage even if we could know it. We have to know how those affected value the damage to be able to assign a price. Consequently, all interested parties must be allowed to bid if the market is to reflect true costs even in its own terms. But neither future generations nor nonhuman species can bid, and of course, poor humans effectively cannot bid.

The cost-internalization model conflates allocation and scale. Getting a price 'right' would help us to reach allocative efficiency as understood within the neo-classical model. But it would not help at all in deciding on whether an economy is of optimal size. Suppose that in 1950 the world had a population of about two billion persons and all its prices were right, and in 2000 a population of about six billion persons and all its prices were right again. We still have no answer to the question of which state of affairs is preferable. From the perspective of the commonwealth of life the human economy is already much too large.

The neo-classical model moves the power of eminent domain – the power to take property with compensation in pursuit of the public good – from the public sector to the private sector. In the United States, for example, after public review and under scrutiny of the court, private property may be taken assuming that just compensation is paid to the person whose property is taken. The right-price model permits the taking of someone else's lungs for private purposes of disposing of air pollution without the safeguards that attend the public exercise of eminent domain. Moreover, there is no assurance that the injured person actually be paid. All the state would have to bring about allocative efficiency would be to collect the necessary taxes to get the price right: there would be no requirement in this model about where the money would be spent.

Society has some goods that it does not wish to sell at any price. One reason is that in many cases these are fiduciary goods, goods that a society sets aside for the benefit of future generations. Examples of these are the Gettysburg National Monument in the United States, the place in Newfoundland where the first transatlantic radio transmission occurred, Stonehenge in the United Kingdom, and the like. We also remove from the market places that are unusual and/or beautiful or both: Victoria Falls or the game herds of the African Savannah.

HOW SHOULD WE THINK ABOUT THE FUTURE?
In stewardship economics there is an explicit class of nondiscountable (and nonsubstitutable) goods grounded in respect for life's common-wealth. In mainstream economics all goods are to be reduced to present discounted values.

Duties in Perpetuity
It is clear that in the case of fiduciary goods discounting is inappropriate. These goods I call the fiduciary structure. Elements of the fiduciary structure are those things necessary for the protection of human rights and the biosphere. These goods include constitutions and wetlands; common law and common property; courts and water courses; fertilizers and fields to put them on. They define the class of things that we hold in common trust.

The Voracious Present

Let's look at the defects of discounting in the context of climate change, a change altering the circumstances of all, or almost all, of life on earth. Here is the way William Nordhaus proposes that we think about the vast changes underway in the earth's energy balance.

> The fundamental assumption we adopt is that policies should be designed to maximize the generalized level of consumption now and in the future. This approach rests on the view that more consumption ... is preferred over less, and in addition that increments of consumption become less valuable as consumption levels increase. In technical terms, these assumptions are embodied by maximizing a social welfare function that is *the discounted sum of the utility of per capita consumption.* [Emphasis added][17]

There are numerous problems with Nordhaus's decision to rely on discounting that are typical of mainstream economics.

Any positive rate of discount assigns lower values to the future than the present. Ironically, if we assume a smooth warming path with slowly accumulating net damage (as these authors do for the most part) then the *adoption* of this framework alone constitutes the decision to do nothing. This is because the benefits of stabilization which occur in the perhaps distant future, say a hundred years, are discounted; while the costs occur in the undiscounted present. *This assures that the goal stated at the Earth Summit in Rio of 'stabilization of greenhouse gas concentrations' will never be met.* The conclusion is such a short inference away from, and so completely determined by, the (unjustified) assumptions of the method that the 'analysis' provided by these authors could be reduced from books to paragraphs.

The authors of this literature ignore Thomas Schelling's criticism that long-term discounting assumes an immortal agent.[18] Surely Schelling is right that there is a world of difference in thinking about my own future consumption and that of others. This difference causes the whole neo-classical framework to collapse for long-term issues of any kind, by conflating issues of allocation (within a lifetime) with those of distribution (between generations). This is completely illegitimate within their own framework, which makes the difference between allocation – distributions of goods or services through properly functioning markets – and distribution issues which correct for markets in the service of equity, fundamental.

Further still, the idea of discounting is far more problematical than normally assumed by neo-classical approaches to climate change. As Derek Parfit has argued,[19] discounting typically confuses things that are correlated with time with time itself. A variety of arguments are offered in support of discounting: risk, opportunity costs, the supposition that future generations will be better off than we are, and so on. But in none of these cases is it time itself that is the key issue. We would think much more clearly about the future if we used a *disaggregated* vocabulary about risk, and opportunity costs; and stated that poorer generations were not obligated to forego their well-being to help those that could be better off, and so on, rather than starting with the assumption the there is *a* social discount rate. Once we see this point, the word 'discounting' could be dropped from our vocabulary as an unnecessary encumbrance for both long-term and proximate issues. Of course, for nonfiduciary goods it makes perfect sense to worry about opportunity costs, risks, relative levels of wealth and the like. Trying to amalgamate all these factors into a single function as discounting tries to obscure rather than clarify these issues.

There are also reasons to doubt that individuals have a rate of time preference; or at least, that it functions in the broad way that economists assume. For example, why must present and future time value be related by an exponential function? Why not some other relationship? The assertion that there is time preference just doesn't accord with common sense. Most of the things I want I don't want right now: it's the wrong time of day, week, or season of my life. I don't want to give my daughter her graduation present until she graduates.

What is referred to as time preference needs to be disaggregated in much the same way as 'the' social discount rate; for instance by the way individuals think about risk and opportunity cost. Once thinking is clarified in this way we are free to see that a person may value the third decade of life equally with the fifth, and drop the encumbering language of time preference as well.[20]

The authors of this literature conflate decisions within a firm or public agency with a program of management for global systems. We need to distinguish between the means to achieve efficiency through markets or their surrogates, and the things that make markets possible – their preconditions. In 'The Cultural Contradictions of Capitalism'[21] Daniel Bell argues that capitalism depends on the very virtues (for example, thrift, hard work, and so on) that it tends to erode. Surely the earth's basic systems such as climate, and the ocean currents, ecosystems, rainfall patterns, and so on that depend on it are candidates for being among market preconditions, yet they are being destabilized by profligate markets, particularly in the energy sector. Of course, it is not just that preconditions of markets that must be constructed, protected, or secured on the fiduciary conception. It is all those things necessary for the protection and enhancement of the three basic rights and the commonwealth of life.

HOW CAN WE GENERATE THE NECESSARY INSTITUTIONS
FOR MARKETS TO OPERATE CORRECTLY?

The steward, the keeper of the earth in perpetuity, must take the long view, be able to step back from markets both to keep them functioning well and to keep them in their place. Mainstream economics focuses on the self-interested actions of individuals in exchanges. Mainstream economics cannot explain how the very institutions necessary to serve either its own macro or micro goals can arise. Markets, according to the mainstream account, depend on things that they do not themselves supply; for example, as we have just seen, on certain virtues such as honesty, saving, and hard work. They depend on antitrust actions (breaking up mono-polies) on the part of government to foster competition, central banks to stabilize the level of economic activity, and the enforcement of contracts to name just a few. Even the limited neo-classical goal of efficiency cannot be achieved without governments capable of imposing cost-internalization instruments (such as Pigovian taxes) so that the market cost of goods reflects their anthropocentric social costs. It requires a set of institutions and persons acting within them who take the long view for markets to operate correctly.

Economists often, in fact, focus on market preconditions. However, this essentially fiduciary behavior (caring for an institution for a very long term) cannot be explained as arising from their own motivational assumptions. Institutional construction is not in any one's short-term interest since it takes away from the pursuit of individual agendas. For this reason, economics *tends* to pay insufficient attention to its own institutional development. The headlong rush to the globalization of 'free' markets has not built the institutional structure necessary to make markets work in a fiduciary sense to begin with. Indeed, globalization is an attempt to evade and undercut those restraining national institutions that we do have. The focus on the margin fails to focus attention on the necessary institutions designed to stabilize currencies, promote employ-ment, and build the necessary public infrastructure for health and trans-portation on which robust economic growth and a healthy society depend.

STEWARDSHIP ECONOMICS CONTRASTED
TO SUSTAINABILITY

As noted in Chapter 1, over the last decade a very large literature has grown up that places the concept of sustainability at the core of thinking about economics, the environment, and future generations. This is certainly a step in the right direction, as it does not depend on the idea of discounting and, hence, recognizes that position in time is not a determinant of moral worth. So, this has begun a useful discussion. But there are a number of reasons for thinking that we should not stop here. First, the sustainability literature says little about *what* should be sustained beyond a concern for needs of the poor. The proliferation of modern weapons may be sustainable, but undesirable, nevertheless. Second, it says little about the *level* at which things should be sustained. Harvesting twenty or fifty bushels of wheat per acre may both be sustainable, but it is not clear, without reference to principles other than sustainability alone, why one should be preferred over another. Third, in most formulations, the standard does little or nothing to protect the more *complex biological communities.* It is often the simplification of those communities to make them productive sources of food that is thought best to serve human needs. Indeed, in Chapter 6 of the Brundtland Report 'Species and Ecosystems: Resources for Development' the protection of other species is justified almost entirely on instrumental grounds. 'Conservation of living natural resources – plants, animals, and micro-organisms, and the nonliving elements of the environment on which they depend – is crucial for development.'[22]

In contrast the commonwealth-of-life conception defines human needs in terms of the three basic rights. It defines both a bottom and upper range for legitimate economic activity. Lastly, it explicitly, and noninstrumentally protects complex communities as essential for life's commonwealth.

OBJECTIONS TO STEWARDSHIP ECONOMICS

There could be a number of objections to stewardship economics. First, it might be claimed that it is not economics at all. Economics, in the eyes of many economists, is simply a description of behavior, how people make choices under conditions of scarcity. It has no normative structure. But both macro- and micro-economics do have normative structures: respectively GDP growth and efficiency. Particularly in the case of macro-economics there is a whole host of institutions which have been designed to facilitate achieving this goal. Stewardship economics simply proposes changing these institutions, which are described in Chapter 7, in service to life's commonwealth.

Second, it could be objected that there is no consensus in favor of the ethical principles derived from the commonwealth of life. But, as argued in this chapter, there is no consensus in favor of the current goals of micro- or macro-economics either. The question is what set of goals is supported by the most convincing reasons, not which ones are the most popular.

Third, it could be argued that stewardship economics pays insufficient attention to employment and wealth creation, which are major public concerns. There is nothing in this framework that would prevent the use of various employment-creating techniques such as monetary and fiscal policy that already exist. Indeed, many of the tools that would be needed to bring about the goals of the commonwealth of life would stimulate employment, such as shifting the tax burden from employment to resource use. This subject is further discussed in Chapter 7.

Nor is stewardship economics against the creation of wealth: indeed it defines the range of legitimate wealth within a broad range. It does not begin with the undemonstrated assumption of the mainstream that resources are necessarily scarce, and desires infinite. Scarcity is not a fact about the world. Numerous societies have existed with a small fraction of our material wealth and perceived themselves to be affluent. There are two ways to be rich – to have a lot and not to need much.[23]

Many in the mainstream believe that there is a positive correlation between money and happiness. But, as Aristotle noted, wealth has negative utility beyond a middle point. We should also be careful to calculate our true wealth, and not assume that economic growth is necessarily bringing more of it. At the very least wealth would have to be adjusted to net out the effects of expenditures that we make to defend ourselves against the untoward effects of economic growth.[24] In addition, it is almost surely one's relative position, once basic needs are met, that influences the level of happiness, not the absolute amount of money someone has. Since aggregate growth cannot increase people's relative position, it may not always increase their happiness.

Fourth, it might be objected that stewardship economics is callous toward human well-being since it places a heavy emphasis on preserving other species. Like economics, so this objection would go, it has two unprioritized objectives that can conflict. In the recasting of morality envisioned herein humans are still at the center. So in the case of genuine conflict between the three basic rights and preserving other species, human well-being – as defined by these rights – would prevail. But it is also important to note that according to the account of human institutions set forth here there are ample *world* resources to secure the three basic rights so that the conflict need not actually arise at the current level of technology, population, and climate.

NOTES

1. In *A Primer for Policy Analysis*, pp. 297–308 Stokey and Zeckhauser list a total of six market failures. These are: imperfect information; transaction costs; nonexistence of markets for some goods; monopolies or oligopolies; externalities; and public goods.

2. Robert Skidelsky, *John Maynard Keynes: Hopes Betrayed 1883–1920*.
3. This definition is taken from David Pearce (ed.), *The MIT Dictionary of Modern Economics*, pp. 297–8.
4. This analysis of the role of Keynesian economics depends on Robert Lekachman, *The Age of Keynes*.
5. I am indebted to Neva Goodwin for suggesting that a metaphor like this would be useful.
6. See Robert Skidelsky, *John Maynard Keynes: Hopes Betrayed*, and *John Maynard Keynes: The Economist as Savior 1920–1937*, pp. 33–9.
7. Herman Daly, *Beyond Growth*, pp. 84–6.
8. John Stuart Mill, *Utilitarianism* in *The English Philosophers from Bacon to Mill*, p. 900.
9. Jeremy Bentham, *Anarchial Fallacies: Being an Examination of the Declaration of Rights Issued during the French Revolution*, vol. 2 of *Works of Jeremy Bentham*, ed. John Bowring, art. II, p. 501.
10. See J. J. C. Smart and Bernard Williams, *Utilitarianism For and Against*, especially pp. 100–7.
11. See The World Bank, *World Development Report 1992*, p. 10–11.
12. C. S. Hollings, 'A Cross-Scale Morphology, Geometry, and Dynamics of Ecosystems,' *Ecological Monographs*, vol. 62, no. 4, 1992, pp. 447–502.
13. Farley Mowat, *Sea of Slaughter*, p. 404.
14. Julian Simon, *Ultimate Resource*.
15. Aldo Leopold, *A Sand County Almanac*.
16. Karl-Henrik Robert, John Holmberg and Karl-Erik Eriksson, 'Socio-ecological Principles for a Sustainable Society,' a paper presented at the International Symposium 'Down to Earth: Practical Applications of Ecological Economics' 24–28 October 1994 in Heredia, Costa Rica.
17. William D. Nordhaus, *Managing the Global Commons: The Economics of Climate Change*, p. 10. Nordhaus discusses no or low cost means of reducing carbon emissions on pages 65–70, but concludes (p. 69) that there is great uncertainty about the relationship between energy use and GDP growth.
18. Thomas C. Schelling, 'Intergenerational Discounting,' *Energy Policy*, 1995, vol. 23, no. 4/5, pp. 395–401.
19. See, Derek Parfit's 'Energy Policy and the Further Future: The Social Discount Rate,' in Douglas MacLean and Peter G. Brown, *Energy and the Future*, pp. 31–7.
20. See, for instance, John Rawl's *A Theory of Justice*, pp. 293–8, for a good discussion of why the idea of time preference is a mistake.
21. See, Daniel Bell, *The Cultural Contradictions of Capitalism*, 1976, pp. 54–60.
22. World Commission on Environment and Development, *Our Common Future*, p. 147.
23. Marshall D. Sahlins, *Stone Age Economics*.
24. Clifford Cobb, Ted Halstead, and Jonathan Rowe. 'If the GDP is Up, Why is America Down?', *The Atlantic Monthly*, October 1995, pp. 59–78.

CHAPTER 4

GOVERNMENT AS TRUSTEE

Political power is that power which every man having in the state of nature has
given into the hands of the society, and therein to the governors whom society
has set over itself with this express or tacit trust.

(John Locke, *Second Treatise*, Chapter XV)

To a revitalized and reconstructed macro economics we must add, in our
quest for a just world order, the concept of government as trustee: a
conception of the state that can properly command our allegiance. The
argument in favor of the trustee model of government is developed in the
following stages: 1) a characterization of the trust model; 2) an account of
the duties of government on the trust model; 3) contrasting it with the neo-
classical conception of state legitimacy; and 4) defending it against
objections.

THE TRUST MODEL

Government as trustee is not, perhaps surprisingly, a quest for a new idea,
but the rediscovery of an old one that has been largely lost to our political
consciousness. This ancient idea – that the government is a trust, that
those who govern are trustees – is what many of us already believe. The
idea that the government is a trustee is well grounded in our political and
philosophical history, particularly in Locke's *Second Treatise*, and it is
Locke's conception with one important modification that I will set forth
here.[1] But the idea was not new with Locke either: its elements are
foreshadowed, for example, in the Magna Carta and Thomas Hobbes'
Leviathan.[2] And the Old Testament concept of the Covenant is an even
more distant precursor. It was part of the general vocabulary of Locke's
contemporaries, probably first appearing in 1556 as an expression of the
obligations of those who rule. It is carried forward by figures as diverse as
Theodore Roosevelt, Gifford Pinchot, John Muir, and Gandhi.

At one level the idea of a trust is partly indeterminate. Certain duties
flow directly from the notion of trusteeship, but by itself it is a fairly

formal concept: we can set up a trust to preserve anything for anyone. To know in detail how governments as trustees should behave, we have to appeal to some underlying moral principles that specify the relevant duties. I have set out and defended what I take to be the appropriate principles in Chapters 1 and 2. The duties set out in Chapter 2, of course, go beyond those familiar to Locke, whose ethic was human centered. Accordingly, the conception of trusteeship defended here is broader. It includes duties to protect and enhance human rights, but also requires that we respect and enhance the commonwealth of life.

Locke writes over and over again of the trust that the people repose in their government, and speaks of those who govern as having a 'fiduciary trust.'[3] For Locke, people seek out government for the

> mutual preservation of their lives, liberties and estates, which I call by the general name, property. The great and chief end, therefore, of men's uniting into commonwealths, and putting themselves under government, is the preservation of their property.[4]

In understanding Locke's theory of government, it is *essential* to keep in mind, as we will see, that 'property' includes *life* and *liberty*, as well as estate. It is important to see that Locke's conception of government takes as one of its central concerns the human propensity for violence. Locke sees his conception of government as an essential way to break the revenge cycles that characterize the state of nature.

The root idea of the trust conception of government is of a fiduciary trust in which the trustee has a duty to preserve and enhance the assets of the trust with a view to the good of the beneficiaries: the citizens. It draws on the general notion that certain persons can be given powers over certain assets to act on behalf of and for the benefit of others. The general duties of the trustees are: 1) to act out of loyalty for the benefit of the beneficiary, not in the trustee's own interests – call this the core feature; 2) not to delegate the entire administration of the trust – call this the accountability feature; 3) to provide the beneficiaries with information concerning the trust – call this the democratic feature; 4) to enforce claims on behalf of the trust – call this the administrative feature; and 5) to make the trust property productive – call this the antiwaste feature.[5] On a trust conception of government, a constitution and laws are the trust documents or instruments. The assets of the trust are the natural-resource base, the coercive powers of the state to tax and to provide for national defense, its legitimate ability to plan, to educate, and in other ways to foster the well-being of both its citizens and the broader commonwealth of life. Corresponding to the trustee's general duties, those who govern must act in the interests of the citizens, not their own interests; perform the duties of office – not delegate them; disclose information to the public; defend the assets of the trust and citizens from unjust interference, destruction and/or waste; and preserve and enhance the assets of the trust.

GOVERNMENT AS TRUSTEE

The trust conception's understanding of government is, then, as follows. First, the trust conception recognizes the direct duty of the government to preserve and enhance the 'property' of all persons. In Locke's conception, as in mine defended here, all persons have obligations to respect the three-way rights of others, including affirmative obligations to secure subsistence rights. The difficulty that the institution of government is designed to solve is the tendency in the state of nature not to discharge these obligations. Government is the default enforcer of both our natural rights *and* natural-law obligations. Those who read Locke as defending only a set of forbearance rights of bodily integrity and freedom of choice completely ignore the natural-law feature of Locke's argument.

Second, the trust model holds that the legislator (and the executive) must discharge these obligations to the public good on the basis of impartial deliberation. It is the obligation of legislators to debate public issues and decide on the public good in light of that debate. Third, the trust conception imposes an obligation to respect human rights. I set out this three-fold conception of rights in Chapter 1.

Fourth, the trust conception explicitly prohibits waste. A trustee's job is the conservation and enhancement of assets and this has direct consequences for action. The fiduciary model recognizes that we have an obligation to leave material resources we find available for our use in a condition at least as good as the one we found them in. In *Second Treatise*, for example, Locke states that a man is entitled to appropriate from the commons whatever he has expended his labor on 'at least where there is enough, and as good left in common for others.'[6] There is a duty to protect and conserve the commons for others including future generations.

Fifth, the fiduciary conception has the capacity to address the special crises of natural resources and biostability we are faced with. Food, water, and clean air are scarce for many people right now. The number of people in the world who are malnourished is in the hundreds of millions. Water for drinking, bathing and irrigation is chronically short in many places. Air pollution is so severe in many third-world cities as to be a major factor in ill health.[7] The trustee model makes these threats to health a central concern by insisting on the preservation of all humanity.

There is now a a *new kind of scarcity*. The very success of industrialized market economies is leading to a scarcity of ecological diversity and stability, and of coherent human communities. Indeed, the problem in some dimensions is not that we will run out of some of the basic inputs of industrialized economies in the intermediate term, but that we won't. Ecological diversity and stability are under threat around the globe from a variety of sources including habitat destruction for housing and commercial development, the harvest of forest products, nonsustainable agriculture, the introduction of exotic species, pesticides and a variety of other sources including destabilization of climate.

The sixth main element of the trustee's duties is that the trustee must respect the virtues of commerce. Securing a robust economy that provides for the needs of persons through trade and agriculture was one of Locke's primary concerns. Indeed much of the *Second Treatise*, written, of course, in a pre-industrial period, is devoted to developing a theory that will ensure that productive resources, particularly agricultural land, will get into the hands of those who will use them productively, a goal that follows directly from Locke's abhorrence of waste. In an age (similar to ours) of uncertain harvests, malnutrition and occasional famines one would hardly expect otherwise. But the ultimate rationale for private appro-priation of the commons is that it serve the common good. On the fiduciary conception, land is not something that can be used simply for the benefit of the present owner, but an asset that must be used for the common good understood in a multi-generational context. It is a community resource. As we will see in the next chapter this view is compatible with the private ownership of real property, but rights of the owner come with the responsibilities of a steward. Private ownership and the market have their place, but in a larger moral framework.

Seventh, Locke's insistence on 'enough and as good left for others' make it explicit that our obligations extend through time. Many theories of state obligation simply ignore the issue, or as we saw in the previous chapter embrace discounting.

THE TRUSTEE AND NEO-CLASSICAL CONCEPTIONS CONTRASTED

We saw in the previous chapter the difficulties associated with resting public policy on an unconstrained utilitarian foundation such as contained in micro-economics. The fiduciary conception avoids these difficulties by resting its conception of state legitimacy on a foundation other than the maximization of utility. Here I want to bring out another contrast. The ability to say what should be traded in the market. In their obsession with the market the proponents of the market failure models of government legitimacy (that government exists to fix markets) gloss over, or perhaps don't even recognize, that *there are certain questions that the market itself is incapable of answering.* By examining the answers given to these questions we uncover levels of discourse that lie deeper than the market. Economists have spent a lot of time on describing the financial requisites of the market, such as money supply and exchange rates. But, as we saw in the previous chapter, they have paid little or no attention to its moral and institutional foundations. Analysis of the functions of the state that is limited to the vocabulary of the market cannot answer fundamental questions that are unavoidable in formulating public policy.

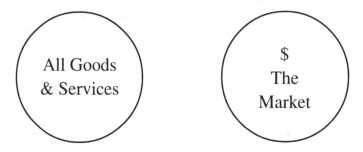

Figure 4.1 All Goods and Services.

Let's begin by depicting markets and all goods and services separately (see Figure 4.1). A strict market-oriented approach to public policy offers no bounds on what should be traded on the market. Since the few responsibilities of the state, like defense, are thought of as market failures we need not represent them separately; once the state has acted the market has been 'corrected' and is thus in theory functioning properly. Merged, the ideal world simply looks like one circle (see Figure 4.2).

Figure 4.2 The Perfect Market.

This picture is very misleading. Many of the toughest questions in public policy involve deciding *what should be for sale*. Political headlines are filled with exactly this range of dispute. Should sex be for sale? All kinds of sex or just some? And sold where? And how? Drugs? If some drugs, which ones and why? Abortions? Public lands? If some public lands, which ones? Medications of questionable usefulness like laetrile? Rights to drill for oil in the Santa Barbara Channel? Should all domestic markets be open to fair foreign competition or only some? How should 'fair' be defined? Should rights to pollute be for sale? Rights to hunt? Attendance at bull fights, or cockfights? Adult pornography? Pornography involving the torture of animals? Prime farmland for a bowling alley? Civil-war battlefields? 'Saturday night' specials? Grenade launchers? Fully automatic weapons? Jet fighters? The United States' Constitution, or the Magna Carta?

What is not now legally for sale? A partial list would include professorships in economics (the irony of this prohibition seems completely to escape some advocates of the market), human beings, many forms of political influence, citizenship, criminal justice, first amendment rights, the right to more than one spouse, exemption from the draft when there is one, jury duty, sex, certain drugs, designated wilderness areas, awards like the Congressional Medal of Honor, organs like eyes, kidneys and hearts, life-threatening items like flammable shirts – and new cars without seatbelts, the right to shoot a bald eagle, the Statue of Liberty, a hired assailant. These are what Michael Walzer in *Spheres of Justice*[8] calls 'blocked exchanges.' A black or grey market exists in many of these areas, but these transactions typically have neither legal nor, in most cases, social sanction. So the situation is now provisionally as in Figure 4.3. But the line between blocked and permitted exchanges is shifting and open to argument. Should babies be for sale? Kidneys?[9] Should we allow concessions in the national parks? Should we legalize prostitution? Many of the important issues of public policy are about what should be bought and sold.

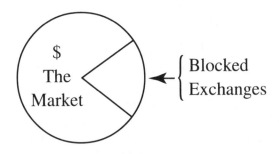

Figure 4.3 Limiting the Market.

And the situation is even more complicated because there are two kinds of blocked exchanges. There are goods which are not legally available at all. Certain drugs and the pelts of some animals that are in danger of extinction are examples of things for which society seeks, for widely accepted reasons, to ensure a supply of zero.[10] And there is another class of 'goods', a supply of which continues to exist but which cannot be bought or sold, for example babies for adoption and organs for transplantation. Here society does not try to reduce the supply to zero, but blocks any market-like transactions. Let's call these two kinds of blocked exchanges respectively, 'prohibited exchanges,' exchanges that are not supposed to take place at all, and 'unpriced exchanges' permitted transactions where purchase and sale are inappropriate means of exchange. In light of these considerations we should revise our diagram (see Figure 4.4).

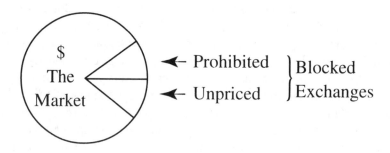

Figure 4.4 How Public Morality Restricts the Market.

By selecting a framework for analysis which *assumes* that markets should operate everywhere the market disciples embrace a principle that is too strong and too shallow. It is too strong in that it assumes that all arguments in favor of blocked exchanges must fail. It is too shallow in that it provides no grounds for deciding, *and even no vocabulary for discussing*, many of the central issues in the real debate: *what transactions should be blocked? What exchanges prohibited? What exchanges priced?* The market itself sheds no light whatsoever on the question of what should be traded in it. But the problem doesn't stop with blocked exchanges.

On what terms should things be for sale? Here, the situation is even more complicated. Many 'market prices' exist in a shadow cast by moral and legal considerations: I will call these penumbral exchanges. The 'true market price' is the price that would be paid by well-informed buyers to well-informed sellers in a perfectly competitive market. Much of what legally can be bought and sold is not sold at its 'true' market price.

To see how far the doctrines we are considering are out of tune with what we actually do, consider the case of money itself. It is not sold, or better rented, at its true market price, which would be the interest rate voluntarily established between lenders and borrowers. On the contrary, interest rates are carefully managed by the Federal Reserve Board to try to stimulate employment while controlling inflation.[11] Charities enjoy government subsidy through their tax-exempt status, and nonprofit franking privileges. Public utility prices are another prime example of prices set on the basis of criteria other than 'true market prices.' Numerous standards *other* than economic efficiency, such as rights to service and avoidance of changes in the status quo determine how prices are actually set.[12] That this is what public-utility commissions actually do doesn't prove that this is what they should do. But it *does* show that for the market disciples to be correct about pricing, *all* other factors must be swept aside. Gas service could be cut off to a home with small sick children. Water rates could be revised drastically if new outlying housing developments made a new reservoir a necessity. As Edward Zajac puts it:

> The closer an institution is to immediate accountability, the less it will be informed by a coherent economic logic and the more by primitive notions of morality and justice.[13]

Whatever the *a priori* logic of the market may dictate there is substantial evidence that responsive public bodies decide on different grounds.

The government's agricultural policy is largely effected by incentive payments. The Soil Conservation Service, for instance, works with farmers to encourage them to engage in agricultural practices that reduce the amount of topsoil lost to erosion. They offer both planning and financial assistance, providing an implicit subsidy to those who participate and altering the true price of farm products.

It should also be noted that churches are in the penumbra. Religious services are not delivered at their true market prices. States and localities subsidize religious institutions by exempting them from property taxes, the federal government by making contributions to religious institutions deductible against income exposed to federal income tax. Similar arrangements exist for private schools and colleges, and the services provided by public schools and universities are obviously delivered to their students at artificially low prices. The list of penumbral prices could obviously go on and on. We need to revise our diagram again (see Figure 4.5).

Here the shallowness of the market-failure conception of public-sector legitimacy comes to the fore again. Their doctrines offer no assistance in deciding what should be in the penumbra or in deciding on the terms governing the transactions that take place within it. Thus a good many other policy topics, such as taxation, public utility pricing, and large aspects of

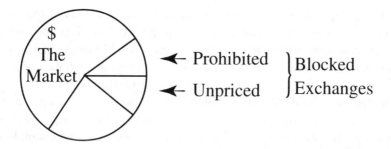

Figure 4.5 Penumbral exchanges: the complexity of public morality.

agricultural policy join blocked exchanges as issues with essential components about which market theorists cannot join real political discourse. The principle is also too strong: from their point of view *all* arguments in support of blocked exchanges of either type and all penumbral exchanges must fail.

Of course, few actually believe that everything should be for sale, or that everything should be sold at its true market price and the literature is beginning to come to grips with this question. Market theorists might also reply that the argument that their principles are too shallow simply ignores much of what they write. Economists regularly discuss problems such as tax exemptions, discounting, income distribution, and the financing of education. But the adjustments to the market failure theory are *ad hoc*; the general, underlying principles go unchallenged, and no alternative *framework* is articulated.

Consider a version of market-failure theory that said simply that everything else being equal there should be a presumption in favor of the market. Or as Friedman puts it, in making a decision we should assign to government intervention extra negative weight.[14] This is really no help at all. When we run into claims that some things should be in the penumbra and that some exchanges should be blocked they include the claim that everything else *isn't* equal. Exchanges are blocked for a variety of reasons. We cannot buy spouses, at least in part for religious reasons. Professorships of economics are not for sale because intellectual qualification, not price, is the relevant distributive criterion. Bribing public officials is prohibited because it is incompatible with democratic principles. Similar nonmarket criteria apply with respect to penumbral exchanges. A floor is put under farm prices to ensure a stable food supply. The poor cannot legally have their heat cut off in the dead of winter because society assumes a responsibility to protect the vulnerable. Churches are subsidized because of the separation of church and state: the state cannot legitimately tax churches because the power to tax is effectively the power to destroy. Saying that there should be a presumption in favor of the market simply sheds no light on the real moral issues underlying pricing and blocked exchanges.

As these examples show, our existing political structures reflect a complex political morality. We appeal to a number of criteria in making our public choices about what is to be in the market, and how goods traded in the market are to be priced. Concepts like need, desert (who is owed what by whom), responsibility, respect, and a vision of the good life all play roles in deciding these questions. The attempt to derive a model of government from economic analysis alone won't work. We need a full-blooded political theory that reflects our complex morality.

Once we see the role of blocked exchanges and penumbral prices we can see clearly that *nothing* in the United States is sold in accordance with free-market principles. Very large numbers of things are bought and sold. Some are very important things like food and housing, where the government intentionally intervenes in the price. The reason that *nothing* is sold at its true market price is that controlled price items have effects on the prices of *other* things. For example, the housing subsidy that the federal government provides through the income-tax deduction of interest affects the price of housing *relative* to the price of washing machines. If having a 'free' market economy means governing oneself in accordance with the precepts of the right then the United States has no such thing. What it does have is a system closer in spirit to the 'just price' conception of the middle ages than to the ideas of market theorists. It would be more accurate to call what exists in the United States a 'Thomistic' market (after St Thomas) than a 'free' market, a formula that would convey the fact that the market rests upon, and exhibits, a complex moral structure. The question is not, as the market devotees would have it, how can we get markets to function with perfect efficiency? It is, rather, what subsidies and other interventions in the market will serve humane and democratic purposes?

The collapse of communist centrally planned economies was not, we can hope, in favor of the 'free' market as the right sees it, or the utilitarian market of the center. Our system is one of indirect central planning of supply and demand. We manage supply in numerous ways that are used to affect prices in areas ranging from the land-grant system of public universities that aims at abundant and low-priced food, to the cutting practices of the Forest Service designed to make lumber available for houses. We manage demand with mechanisms ranging from fiscal and monetary policy to food stamps. The difference between the defunct centrally planned economies and the existing democratic regimes is thus much less sharp than is widely supposed. Through a long process the industrial democracies have found that it works to manage supply and demand indirectly and centrally to reach democratically determined social objectives. Their reaction to the disaster of 19th-century capitalism took a different course than that proposed by Marx; but it discarded utopian markets just the same.

DEFENDING THE TRUST CONCEPTION

The trust conception presents an alternative vision to current ways of thinking about domestic politics, and our obligations through time. But it is tempting to dismiss it as a utopian scheme – desirable, but unworkable.

First, it might be argued that it is not possible to adequately motivate the trustee him- or herself. Second, its universal duties stretching across time could be thought to require too much sacrifice. Third, it may appear that a trustee government has so many duties that it would require large and interventionist bureaucracies. Last, it could be objected that the trustee conception is incompatible with the preservation of fundamental liberties.

MOTIVATING THE TRUSTEE

The market model has an account of how the self-interested motivation of private individuals can work for the common good through exchange. In contrast, the trust conception appears to *lack a theory about how to motivate the trustee*. Indeed, seen from the perspective of the market it appears to require actions – to promote the well-being of others – that cannot be motivated. Here, as elsewhere when the self-interest hypothesis is invoked, it is vital not to concede the initial dichotomy between self-interest and altruism. An institution founded solely on altruism would be unstable at best. Rather, it is better to turn to the question into: *which* self do I want to serve? Assuming a role creates new self-definitions of identity. One way to understand the motivation of the trustee is to compare her to other familiar professionals. Physicians are supposed to place the well-being of patients ahead of their own interests, and we have no problem in condemning those who have conflicts of interests such as the ownership of diagnostic centers to which they unnecessarily refer their patients. The issue is how we get professionals to interpret their self-understanding and therefore their self-interest in a way that stresses the duties built into their role.

The trustee acts in the public interest because she accepts such action as her role obligation, just as physicians act in the interests of patients. Those who seek public office, either elected or appointed, are motivated by honor – by the approbrium of their fellows. And we pay this homage as a way of reinforcing the connection between their role to act in our interest and their interest. By addressing elected officials as 'the honorable,' for instance, we reinforce the internal integrity of public servants as professionals. Perhaps it would make economists happy to refer to this homage as the price we pay for the integrity of our public servants.

EXCESSIVE DUTIES

Another class of objections might hold that *in a variety of ways the trust model requires too much*: that it is too disruptive of our individual lives and plans by requiring excessive concern with the preservation of others. It is startling to note that the other-regarding aspects of the trustee conception are extremely modest when compared to the underlying moral assumptions of market-based models. The centrist-market model finds its roots in classical utilitarianism, whose defects we considered in Chapter 3. Recall that utilitarianism requires that we seek the greatest happiness of the greatest number. The market school accepts this obligation and then falsely claims that the obligations can be discharged indirectly through voluntary exchanges. Note how strong the requirement is that *happiness* be maximized. It requires that our own projects and purposes always be subject to revision or cancelation if we could thereby achieve more happiness overall. If we are seeking something with a more modest account of our obligations to others, the trustee concern with only the *preservation* of all is far preferable. Ironically, the market account which often seems so selfish is, at bottom, altruistic in the extreme.

BIG BROTHER GOVERNMENT

It might appear, on the other hand, that the trustee conception *permits too much*. One version of this objection might be that the model asserts so many duties that it paves the way for a large bureaucratic state that intervenes in the lives of the citizens in too many ways. This objection is without force with respect to either ends or means. The trust conception does not place our civil and religious liberties in jeopardy – these rights are built into it from the beginning. Protecting them is the most fundamental duty of the trustee, captured in the US Constitution in the Bill of Rights: liberty of religion, speech and association, due process, and protection against unreasonable search and seizure. In cases of conflict between the will of the people as expressed through the legislature and rights, rights trump.

The objection also ignores the flexibility of means available to the trustee. The model does not, for example, condemn the market. Indeed one of the duties of the trustee is to ensure that markets operate efficiently in their proper sphere. The market and the incentives that it captures are among the many instruments available to the trustee. Trusteeship does not demand large public bureaucracies. It is perfectly pragmatic along this dimension and because of the duty to use the taxpayer's money with care, it moves in the direction of parsimonious government. Hence the trustee should discharge its fiduciary duties in the most effective manner possible. As we will see in the next chapters it can rely as readily on tax incentives, on privatization of public services, or market-oriented demand subsidies, if these steps will discharge its responsibilities most efficiently.

The trustee conception is not radically egalitarian, favoring large income or other resource transfers to those who are not productive members of society. While the concept of 'preserving all mankind' recognizes the moral worth of all persons it does not command us to provide each person with equal monetary income. There are clear obligations *to* the poor because of their vulnerability, and clear limits on those obligations. There are clear obligations *of* the poor to become productive members of society and to share in the obligations of citizenship.

Ironically, it is the market model that permits too much, both by government and by individuals. In assuming that our obligations to one another can be discharged through mutually self-interested exchange it contains no account of what we owe our contemporaries at home or abroad; nor does it provide a satisfactory account of our obligations to future persons, or to the broader commonwealth of life. In failing to recognize, much less deal with, the dependence of the economy on the biosphere the market model offers no assurance that we have not already dangerously overloaded the biosphere, and it legitimates the destruction of the broader community of life, of which we are a part.

TRUSTEESHIP AND LIBERTY

Last, I reply to the objection that it unduly limits freedom. My responses are (1) no social arrangement allows unrestricted liberty; (2) failure to intervene also restricts liberty – the United States and other nations that emit lots of carbon are imposing a new climate regime on the world without the consent of billions worldwide; (3) by preserving assets the trust conception increases the choices that future persons have; (4) by emphasizing the obligation of the government to develop the capacity for choice for the present generation it increases our freedom; and (5) the loss of negative (absence of interference) freedom on the part of some people is offset by the increase in positive (having the means to act) liberty on the part of others.

NOTES

1. Both Nozick and Epstein (see note 4, Chapter 1) claim that their theories are grounded in Locke. Neither reading is credible. Historically, they take only a portion of Locke's conception of natural rights and ignore entirely the requirements of natural law. Besides completely undercutting their claims to historical authority this also commits them to all the mistakes of a voluntaristic account of obligations. They completely miss the Janus-faced aspect of

contract theory: that we enter into the contract because of our vulnerability. Even in contract theory itself it is the vulnerability, not the promise, that is foundational.

In addition, in order to block redistribution, both use the argument that all actions of the state must be unanimous. But as Ian Shapiro has noted in *The Evolution of Rights in Liberal Theory*, this requirement backfires since if some people want redistribution the minimum state does not enjoy unanimous support either.

There is a symmetry in the inadequacies of contemporary theories of the state. Those on the right such as Nozick's and Epstein's fail to provide any account of the duties of the rich. Those on the left, like Rawl's as set out in *A Theory of Justice*, fail to provide any account of the obligations of the poor. The trustee conception grounds the obligations of both.

2. See J. W. Gough's 'Political Trusteeship' in his *John Locke's Political Philosophy* (Oxford: Clarendon Press, 1973) pp. 154–92 for a discussion of the widespread use of this concept before and subsequent to Locke. See also John Dunn's 'The Concept of "Trust" in the Politics of John Locke' in Richard Rorty, et al., *Philosophy in History*, pp. 279–301 for a discussion of human trustworthiness in Locke's thought.

3. John Locke, *Second Treatise*, para. 156.

4. John Locke, Ibid., para. 124.

5. This account of the duties of the trustee is taken, with modifications, from *Putting the Public Trust Doctrine to Work* prepared by David C. Slade, Esq. Obtained from the Coastal States Association. Published November 1990.

6. John Locke, *Second Treatise*, para. 27.

7. See the World Resources Institute, *1998–99 World Resources: Environmental Change and Human Health* for data on and explanations of these trends.

8. Michael Walzer, *Spheres of Justice: A Defense of Pluralism*, p. 100.

9. See Susan Hankin Denise's 'Regulating the Sale of Human Organs' in *Virginia Law Review*, vol. 71, no. 6, September 1985, pp. 1015–38, for a discussion of the present state of the law on this subject. In general, organs may not legally be sold.

10. Seventh Annual Meeting of the Conference of Parties for the Convention on International Trade of Endangered Species of Wild Fauna and Flora, held 9–20 October 1989. US Fish and Wildlife Service.

11. See Milton Friedman, *Capitalism and Freedom*, Chapter 3, especially p. 55, for Friedman's discussion of the role of the state in controlling the money supply.

12. See, for instance, Edward E. Zajac, 'Perceived Economic Justice: The Example of Public Utility Regulation' in H. Peyton Young (ed.), *Cost Allocation: Methods, Principles, Applications*, pp. 119–53.

13. Ibid., p. 123.

14. Friedman, *Capitalism and Freedom*, p. 32.

CHAPTER 5

CIVIL SOCIETY AND THE COMMONWEALTH OF LIFE

> Instead of presuming that ... individuals sharing a commons are inevitably
> caught in a trap from which they cannot escape, I argue that the capacity of
> individuals to extricate themselves from various types of dilemma situations
> varies ... Institutions are rarely either private or public – 'the market' or 'the state.'
> (Elinor Ostrom, *Governing the Commons*)

Defeating or mitigating the common enemies of humanity, disease,
famine/malnutrition, violence, unjustified taxes, and corrupt authority,
requires a number of instruments: a portfolio of means. We must avoid
the simplistic and dangerous notion that the only two alternatives before
us for improving the human condition and protecting the commonwealth
of life are the state or the market. The twentieth century was ravaged by
war, and characterized by the nearly global rending of the fabric of life.
We have a compelling obligation to find alternatives to utopian markets
and autocratic states.

Many of the seeds of reconstruction have begun to sprout – albeit in
disparate gardens. As Karl Polanyi noted in the 1940s in his idea of the
'double movement' as human activity gets more and more oriented
around markets, devices spring up to protect nature, human labor/human
beings more generally, and money itself from market forces. This double
movement is now underway around the globe. In the current iteration it
seeks to protect us and the rest of nature from both the state and the market
– the twin tyrannies of our age. Human-rights groups are largely oriented
to protecting against excesses of the state, though as global markets
progressively weaken states, and capital becomes more and more influential in the manner states behave, market forces become threats to human
rights. In some nations a resurgent but still weak union labor movement
tries to protect human beings from the market. Yet with hundreds of
millions unemployed in a globalizing labor market it is difficult to be
optimistic about the resurgence of strong labor unions. Environmental
groups in the former Soviet Bloc seek to redress state abuses of nature. In
the Americas we are concerned with misuses of nature flowing from the

market. At the same time, state mismanagement of public resources such as forests, along with ineffective regulation of other resources from fisheries to forests, is widespread. The role of the central banks in managing the money supply and interest rates is now widely, nearly universally, taken for granted. The purpose of this management, as we saw in Chapter 3, is social stability.

What is needed, and what this book seeks to provide, is a frame of reference by which to pull together and strengthen these forces by protecting basic rights from both the state and the market and, what is the focus of this chapter, fostering the stewardship of the commonwealth of life.

In this chapter I will first argue that we have mischaracterized the options before us as a choice between the state and the market. Second, I define civil society, and its general role in mediating between state and market. Third, I lay out the characteristics of a civil society that would protect and enhance the commonwealth of life. This conception of civil society will lead to finding a central, but contextual and subordinate, role for private property within a fiduciary framework. Last, objections to a stewardship conception of private property are considered.

RICOCHETING BETWEEN STATE AND MARKET

The twentieth century has ricocheted, with disastrous results, between state and market. To somewhat arbitrarily fix a date the seeds of present dilemma were laid down during the English experiment with self-regulating markets that began with the repeal of the poor laws in 1834. The utopian market regime and the attendant social havoc of that era inspired a corresponding and even more destructive utopian fantasy. Marx gave us the idea that the only way to protect ourselves from the excesses of the market was to place it fully under government control. This legitimated the widespread tyrannies that are just now in the process of collapse. Hitler arose, by a process of election, allegedly to save the German people from the disastrous results of the great depression and the civil unrest that characterized Germany in the 1920s and 1930s. Thus Communists and Nazis alike arose in response to failures of the market utopia. The abuses and blunderings of the Nazis and Communists, in their war-making proclivities, their centrally controlled economies, and their lack of respect for human rights were legion, and we are well rid of them.

We have now ricocheted back to 'markets and democracy' bringing upon ourselves, and the hapless creatures with whom we share this planet, another iteration of the failed utopian scheme of the nineteenth century: the perfectly functioning market. This time the scheme is dressed up, to be sure, with the Keynesian inventions of the central banks and clad in the progeny of Bretton Woods: the World Bank and the International Monetary Fund. The World Trade Organization has been established to move the world in the direction of perfectly competitive markets. Yet there is a big gap between rhetoric and reality. We are fortunate indeed not to have 'free markets' with all their attendant instabilities. As we have just seen in Chapter 4, in the United States, the primary exporter of the idea of 'free markets' there is nothing for sale at a price that is set solely by buyers and sellers.

If the Nazis and the Communists are to be rejected because of too much centralized power in government and its rampant abuse; we have now embraced a paradox. Immense power over humans and nonhumans alike is now concentrated in the hands of capital. Yet there is no reason to think of conspiracy, or even substantial co-ordination, among the rich. Their minions in government, the universities and think tanks are hard at work arranging the world in their service. The unity in service to utopian markets is doctrinal. It is, as we saw in Chapter 3, a collection of metaphors that does not offer a satisfactory account of what it is for, where it is, how to think about the side effects of processes, how much is enough, how to think about time, or its own institutional assumptions.

Nor is the democracy part of the equation in a healthy state. The very country in the process of exporting 'free markets and democracy,' the United States, has declining participation in its elections, and widespread collapse of public belief in the legitimacy of government. In those countries without laws regulating expenditures on campaigns the processes of government itself have become subordinate to market incentives. In an irony that escapes most observers the chief purveyors of markets and democracy to the world have neither.

WHAT CIVIL SOCIETY IS AND WHAT IT IS FOR

The development and implementation of stewardship economics and trustee governments would be substantial steps toward fulfilling the requirements of an ethic grounded in the idea of the commonwealth of life. But even taken together they are insufficient to the task at hand. Furthering the progress project requires a third set of institutions to hold the market and the state accountable. This is the cluster of institutions we have come to call civil society. I start by defining civil society and then describe its functions.

CIVIL SOCIETY DEFINED

Civil society ... refers to collective interaction taking place above the individual and independent from the state and resulting in a sense of allegiance and societal norms. Thus, a central aspect of this notion of civil society is the constitution of a space for collective life outside the direct purview of the state and yet partially responsible for generating and defining social life.[1]

The idea of civil society is normally associated with institutions between state and market that exist within a given polity. In all societies there are the churches, charities, associations, clubs, rites of passage, and so on by which individuals define themselves in terms of common purposes of protection, the expression and sharing of grief, joys, interests, and pleasures.

WHAT CIVIL SOCIETY DOES

Civil society serves at least two functions. First, it serves to check excesses of the market, and of government. It serves as a balance wheel. This element seeks an equilibrium. Second, it, along with the government and the market, plays a subordinate role in an overall agenda of progress. This element gives direction.

Balancing Power

For reasons just given, there should a system of checks and balances among the state, the market, and civil society. Each serves to strengthen, shape, direct, and prevent abuses of the other. The state must act to check an undue tyranny of money. For example, good public policy prevents subordinating the goals of medicine to the forces of the market; and at the same time maintains a patent system to provide market stimuli for the invention of new drugs. It thus helps to protect and foster the goals of a central institution of civil society: the institutions and ethics of the medical profession. Conversely, the state works to protect the market. Decentralized and efficient markets – as defined by the first kind of efficiency (maximizing the satisfaction of desire) – are possible only with aggressive, even persistent, state action. Further, the central banks serve to mitigate the fluxes of the business cycle aiming for prosperity and social stability.

Conversely, markets work to check the undue concentration of power in the hands of government, to stimulate invention, enhance liberty, and create wealth. The market stands as a citadel against the overreaching state which seeks to gather undue power. When the state becomes indifferent, tyrannical, or unresponsive, the market serves to check it by creating alternative centers of power and influence.[2] There is, of course, the danger that the independence of government will be undercut as it has been in the United States by making election to public office dependent on raising large sums from the very sources government should be regulating. The market can also serve to foster or undercut civil society. New products stimulate new forms of association, new foci of interest. Numerous inventions of the last centuries have enhanced communication, and fostered a healthy and diverse civil society. On the other hand, the centrifugal, atomistic, forces of the market can serve to undercut many of the institutions of civil society. Distant labor markets have hastened the demise of many a rural church.

The institutions that make up civil society provide a third foci of power. Many institutions of civil society are created expressly for the purpose of influencing government, or have this as a major purpose. Civil society directly influences government simply by existing. It shapes the terms of discourse, and directs the energy of citizens along certain paths. Private foundations accumulate resources and use them for purposes that further, or are at cross purposes with, those of government. Governments are urged to promote the arts, protect human rights, cut or raise taxes, make available or prevent abortions, and so on. Civil society also influences and aims to influence the market. Professional associations set standards of entry to the professions. Churches and numerous civic institutions work to prevent such deleterious actions as the advertising of cigarettes to the selling of land mines.

Giving Direction

The relations between civil society, government, and the market need to be regrounded in the progressive agenda of relief from famine/malnutrition, violence, unjustified taxes, and corrupt authority set in the context of the commonwealth of life. We have a portfolio of means that can be used in pursuit of these objectives, a way of shaping institutions to move in this direction. In this way the idea of progress against these common enemies serves as the north star toward which to aspire.

Here are some examples of how it works by at once checking and directing our institutions. The institutions of agriculture, police and the armed forces, medicine, public administration and the like are subordinate activities justified by our common progressive purposes. Each must participate in the market, each must stand apart from it. Each depends upon, yet goes beyond, government. The bricks and mortar which go into hospitals have to be bought, and the doctors and nurses who work in them have to be paid. At the same time the practice of medicine adheres to a set of norms based in the good of the patient derived from the society of physicians and codified by government. Similarly, public members of the police force have to be trained, clothed, and paid, but their services are not properly bought and sold in the market. Though agricultural products are, of course, sold in the market we also recognize and attempt to foster stewardship on the part of farmers. Doctors, police, and farmers alike all have robust 'fraternal' societies that exist in the space between state and market.

CONSTRUCTING A CIVIL SOCIETY FOR STEWARDSHIP

Once we extend our concerns to the commonwealth of life our expectations from markets, government, and civil society become broader, and their evaluation is seen from a fresh perspective. It is often argued that marketable private-property rights or complete control by government are, respectively, the best way to preserve the resource base. Neither arrangement, taken alone, will protect the commonwealth of life. Let's start with marketable private-property rights.

MARKETABLE PRIVATE-PROPERTY RIGHTS

This school of thought typically begins with what Garrett Hardin has mischaracterized as the tragedy of the commons.[3] As we will see shortly *common* property resources do not necessarily suffer degradation for often communities form to protect them. Hardin's argument applies more accurately to property which is *unowned*.

From this point of view unowned property – whether it is land, water, air, trees or wildlife – is prone to exploitation and degradation. The root idea is that each person gets 100 per cent of the benefits of what they extract from the unowned asset, but suffer only a portion of the loss of the degraded resource. For example, people who take fire wood from a public forest get all the wood they procure, but only suffer indirectly and marginally from less wood in the future, increased erosion, siltation, insufficient aquifer recharge, and other results of resource depletion. Similar considerations apply to the disposal of undesirable waste in a common such as air or water. Individuals who dispose of it get rid of what they do not want, and suffer only a small portion of the degradation of the medium in question. The factory gets rid of all its unwanted smoke and suffers only as much as others from increased air pollution. So in a system where property is unowned there is a tendency to run down the resources.

The proposed remedy is to convert the unowned resource into one that is owned: to establish private-property rights.[4] The idea of private-property rights has three elements: exclusion, use, and disposition. Those who favor this solution advocate strong interpretations of each of these terms. Take exclusion: the right to keep other people, and the undesirable side effects of their activities off the property. This is the source of antitrespass laws, and the basis of some of the controls we have over pollution which may move from one property to another. A second element is use: the right to use the property as one wishes. To cultivate, to harvest, to build, to strip of resources, whatever the owner may wish providing his or her uses do not interfere with the uses by others of their property. The third element is disposal. The owner has the right to pass on the property as he or she wishes by gift, sale, or other means, to whomever he or she wishes.

The basic argument of this school of thought is that establishing these rights will create incentives for the conservation of resources because the owner will not wish to degrade something he or she owns. It is an essential element of this perspective that the rights be marketable so that owners can reap the benefits from their property when they no longer wish to, or can, own it. This maximizes, so the argument goes, the incentive for care of the resource. Property rights should be established over real property such as land. This is the central case where someone may fence or otherwise signal that the property in question is for their own exclusive use. For example, a farm posted with 'No trespassing' signs. Property rights may also be established over a fishery by the establishment of tradeable quotas for a certain number of tons of fish, or a marketable license to operate a fishing boat in certain waters. Property rights may also be established with respect to pollution, by the creation of tradeable permits to pollute.

A look at the history of how this idea of private property plays out is contained in William Cronon's *Changes in the Land*.[5] Cronon depicts the nearly complete transformation of the New England landscape by the English settlers, through the establishment of agriculture and forestry. The European system of property rights along with other factors, most particularly disease, simply extirpated, subordinated or drove from the land and water scapes the pre-existing civilization and much of the flora and fauna. The English conception of property rights described above replaced the Native American conception of usufruct rights: the rights to use the fruits of land without substantially altering it. The Native American system had no rights of exclusion except of people not in the tribe, or who had not been granted permission to come on the land to hunt and/or gather. Rights of use included the taking of game, the establishment of small settlements, and small-scale agriculture that moved on as the soil was depleted. No individuals had rights of disposition since the land was thought to belong to the tribe in common.

Cronon's history and many others show that the idea of establishing property rights by itself is unlikely, except by the most fortunate of coincidences, to conserve the existing resources. If the owner's preferences happen to coincide with the conservation or restoration of resources fine and good. There have certainly been a few cases where this has been true, such as that of Aldo Leopold himself in the management of his farm. But the overall tendency associated with the English conception of property rights is what Joseph Sax has called 'transformative.'[6] In the English system, and this was certainly a point emphasized by Locke, legitimate title to property is obtained by transforming it from its natural to a 'useful', or productive, state. Within the mainstream conception of property rights as advocated by the 'privatization' solution to environmental degradation there is no place for the duty, though no explicit prohibition either, to conserve natural communities. These duties, when they are recognized at all, are supposed to be discharged by the public in a system of parks and wildlife refuges.

Markets for real property by themselves *tend* to undercut the long-term maintenance of the commonwealth of life for a variety of reasons. Individuals may have short-time horizons whereas the commonwealth of life typically requires forbearance, care, and restoration – which mix of these depends on the circumstances – in perpetuity. People may extract profits and then move on. Carelessness with land and the life on it is extremely common in many societies. Individual property owners are often unaware of and/or indifferent to systems effects of their actions. In some cases, such as in property-rights movements, they are overtly hostile to suggestions that they have obligations with respect to property other than the satisfaction of their own desires. Many of the resources we are interested in protecting, for example migratory birds, do not lend themselves to the establishment of property rights necessary for the functioning of markets. It is interesting to note that creating absolute property rights of the sort advocated by this school would have to move us in the direction of materials internalization since any pollution that affects another's property is a violation of their right to it. Carried to an extreme, as it is in this way of thinking, this idea of private property falls into self-contradiction once we recognize the extreme interconnectedness of things. When my neighbor fills his bathtub from the common aquifer under our property, he takes from me. Absent complete materials internalisation (keeping all effects of what I do on my own property), if my rights to property really entitle me to exclude everything you do on your property which would effect me, neither of us has any use rights at all.

LEVIATHAN

Looked at historically the private-property solution to the degradation of the commons has been tried and failed. The wholesale destruction of much of the forest cover of the United States led Gifford Pinchot to found the United States Forest Service. Pinchot was successful in placing large amounts of land in the western United States in a system of National Forests to be used by the public for a variety of purposes including logging, recreation such as hunting and fishing, water retention and purification, and erosion control.

But government ownership or control by itself is not the solution either. Much can be learned from the arguments of the private-property school. Government agencies often become 'captured' by the industries and individuals most interested in short- or medium-term exploitation of the resource. Those wishing to harvest timber on public lands often have the time, money, and influence to get the regulators to act favorably on their requests. Governments are often remote from the sites in need of care and management. In large countries bureaucracies may be separated by thousands of miles from the resources they are supposed to manage. As a result information is hard to get, and often even harder to interpret. The incentives of public servants may or may not coincide with the long-term well-being of the resource that they are given to protect. They may define themselves and their interests more in terms of their advancement in the bureaucracy than in relation to the protection of the resource. For these reasons the rush to government control of resources is an imperfect solution at best. The degradation of much of the public land in North America is a stark and depressing testimony to the failure, in many cases, of public management as a means of preserving the resource base.

A FIDUCIARY CIVIL SOCIETY

A mixed system with civil society at its core appears to be the best at preventing the degradation of the commonwealth of life. In her seminal *Governing the Commons* Elinor Ostrom has defined a common pool resource as follows:

> The term 'common pool resources' refers to a natural or man-made resource system that is sufficiently large as to make it costly (but not impossible) to exclude potential beneficiaries from obtaining benefits from its use. To understand the process of organizing and governing CPRs, it is essential to distinguish between the *resource system* and the flow of *resource units* produced by the system, while still recognizing the dependence of the one on the other.[7]

A common pool resource (CPR) can be a fishery, a forest, the Internet, the air, the oceans, the ecological health of a stream, and so on. In all these cases and many, many more resources *units* can be appropriated by individuals without regard to the health of the *system*. For example, fish may be taken from a stream at a rate which exceeds the growth efficiency of the overall fishery, or methods of extraction may impair the ecological efficiency of the system by causing substantial collateral damage. Similarly, waste may be discharged at a rate or in a manner that degrades the resource.

Ostrom has identified eight characteristics of institutions that are successful in protecting common pool resources (see Table 5.1). Markets, private property, and government may all have roles to play in a successful system. Individuals associated with CPRs respond to market forces though the kinds of things they harvest and the prices they receive.

Table 5.1 Design principles illustrated by long-enduring CPR institutions

1. Clearly defined boundaries
   Individuals or households who have rights to withdraw resource units from the CPR must be clearly defined, as must the boundaries of the CPR itself.

2. Congruence between appropriation and provision rules and local conditions
   Appropriation rules restricting time, place, technology, and/or quantity of resource units are related to local conditions and to provision rules requiring labor, material, and/or money.

3. Collective-choice arrangements
   Most individuals affected by the operational rules can participate in modifying the operational rules.

4. Monitoring
   Monitors, who actively audit CPR conditions and appropriator behavior, are accountable to the appropriators or are the appropriators.

5. Graduated sanctions
   Appropriators who violate operational rules are likely to be assessed graduated sanctions (depending on the seriousness and context of the offense) by other appropriators, by officials accountable to these appropriators, or by both.

6. Conflict-resolution mechanisms
   Appropriators and their officials have rapid access to low-cost local arenas to resolve conflicts among appropriators or between appropriators and officials.

7. Minimal recognition of rights to organize
   The rights of appropriators to devise their own institutions are not challenged by external governmental authorities.

For CPRs that are parts of larger systems:

8. Nested enterprises
   Appropriation, provision, monitoring, enforcement, conflict resolution, and governance activities are organized in multiple layers of nested enterprises.

Source: Elinor Ostrom, *Governing the Commons: The Evolution of Institutions for Collective Action*, p. 90.

There can be tradeable extraction and disposal rights. In some systems there may be ownership of real property. For example, property along a river might be owned, but rights to take from the river or dispose of things in it would be subject to community definition and oversight.

The role of government is also crucial as noted in numbers five and six. Government can provide an ultimate set of sanctions for controlling rogue behavior when that behavior is not susceptible to the instruments available to the monitors or the more directly involved community. For example, the process may begin with requests for changed behavior. This may be followed by calling public attention to the nonconforming behavior, and the application of informal sanctions to the offending party. Fines may be levied, the person may be ostracized for their behavior, and the like. But on occasion these tools are insufficient. Here the role of government as the enforcer of last resort is crucial. The civil and criminal powers of the state have definite roles to play producing sanctions of sufficient force to bring some rogues into line. A parallel role may be played by the state in offering opportunities for dispute resolution. Of course, informal mechanisms for resolving differences may evolve, and would often be preferable to the more cumbersome techniques of the courts. But a court system standing in the background may well be crucial in keeping a CPR well functioning.

The point of a system such as Ostrom's is that there is a group of persons who are concerned with the conservation of the resource. They set up standards of behavior along with informal and formal means to enforce those standards. Within these systems markets, private property, and government all play important roles.

PRIVATE PROPERTY

Paradoxically perhaps, many, but not all of the traditional arguments for the institution of private property survive within a framework of the commonwealth of life. In *Anarchy, State, and Utopia* Robert Nozick summarizes these as follows:

> [I]t increases the social product by putting means of production in the hands of those who can use them most efficiently (profitably); experimentation is encouraged, because with separate persons controlling resources, there is no one person or small group whom someone with a new idea must convince to try it out; private property enables people to decide on the pattern and types of risks they wish to bear, leading to specialized types of risk bearing; private property protects future persons by leading some to hold back resources from current consumption for future markets; it provides alternative sources of employment for unpopular persons who don't have to convince any one person or small group to hire them, and so on.[8]

In the context of the commonwealth of life, as it was in Locke's natural-law framework, private property is a subordinate institution. It is to be judged on instrumental grounds. Historical evidence weighs in heavily on the side of private property as a key factor in the discharge of fiduciary duties during the centuries that we assumed that obligations were exclusively, or primarily, to persons. One of the brilliant features of Locke's theory was its endorsement of the *transformative* value feature of property rights. We gain rights to property, in Locke's view, as we have seen by the mixing of our labor with nature in a manner that allows appropriation from the commons that leaves 'enough and as good for others.' It is the transformation of nature that confers extra benefits on him- or herself and the rest of humanity. In the *Second Treatise* Locke wrote: 'God and his reason commanded him to subdue the earth, i.e., improve it for the benefit of life, and therein lay out something upon it that was his own, his labor.'[9]

Patent medicines derived from naturally occurring substances are instrumental in saving millions around the world from disease through vaccination and the treatment of disease. The ability to own what one has produced has undoubtably helped to create incentives to invent numerous labor-saving devices from pumps to electricity that have released millions from back-breaking drudgery. History amply demonstrates that a private-property system in agricultural land is a crucial element in highly productive agriculture and the elimination of famine and food shortages in many parts of the globe. Forest-stewardship programs promote the production of wood and fuel from woodlands and at the same time conserve and enhance habitat for numerous species, cleanse streams and air, help to recharge aquifers, provide for recreation, and the like.

Private property also has a fiduciary function within an ethic of the commonwealth of life. The private-property owner acts as a steward on behalf of the rest of life. The question: what is the maximum return I can get for this property? is not central and in many cases not even relevant. The question is what is the role of this property in the celebration and support of life?

It is useful to contrast this conception with alternative conceptions of the nature of human property rights in land, which I use as a surrogate for nature generally. These rights can be clustered in at least three great classes. In each of these classes property rights are concerned with three things: exclusion; use; and disposition. As we have seen, each of these specifies a legal rule and often a social expectation, which may or may not coincide with the legal rule with respect to these three factors. Exclusion is the right to determine who or what may enter into or on to the property in question. For instance, antitrespass laws constitute a legal right to keep others from property. Rights of use permit the owner to determine what activities he or she will undertake on the property: to farm for wheat, grow trees, fill or drain, build houses or commercial structures. Rights of disposal refer to the ability to transfer the property to others by gift or sale without restriction.

PROPERTY AS RIGHTS

The three conceptions of property have interpretations of these three components. One of them, what I will call the *property as rights* conception stresses that there are rights to property of the three sorts set out above that, in its logically pure form, are absolute. The *property as rights* conception underlies much of public opinion in the United States, particularly in rural areas where it is taken as axiomatic that if someone owns property one may do what one wishes with it, when one wants to do it. If someone owns a gravel pit that discharges sediment into a public lake attempts to control or eliminate the sedimentation are seen, in this framework, as an interference with the rights of the gravel-pit owner. Fortunately few actually believe this. Rather, it constitutes a pole on a continuum where the rights of owners to exclude, use, and dispose of property are at their sole discretion.

The other end of the spectrum, defining the other end of the logical possibilities, holds that all private property, except perhaps for personal items like clothing, are illegitimate. This is the position of writers like Karl Marx who saw private property as a means for the owners of capital to exploit the workers. In this framework property is theft.

It is evident that neither pole defines a reasonable place from which to frame one's conception of the right to property. The property-rights conception is incompatible with property rights at all once one recognizes the interpenetrating character of natural and human practices. If there is an absolute right of exclusion there are few, if any, rights of use. For a fire in my neighbor's wood stove inevitably will mean smoke in my yard, and in my lungs. The property as rights conception thus becomes a form of theft of the property of others. Thus in its pure version the *property as rights* conception falls into self-contradiction. In practice this conception means that property owners have rights unless there are explicit prohibitions to the contrary either in the law or in social custom. The other end of the continuum is not a reasonable place to be either. It is incompatible with the idea of progress since it is unable to harness the creative features of the institutions of property set out in Nozick's summary above.

PROPERTY AS A PUBLIC TRUST

The property as a public trust conception looks on property as a bundle of rights and duties to other persons. It has two versions: the forbearance version, and the resource version of the public trust. The forbearance version states property rights as those rights which we have to do as we wish with respect to exclusion, use, and dispositions just so long as we respect the similar rights of others. This is the traditional and in my view mistaken interpretation of Locke. It is cognizant of the multiple ways in which property uses interact and tries to strike a balance between competing uses of owners in a way which will preserve the progressive features of the idea of property. On this view the unregulated use of property constitutes theft since it permits one person to take from another without limit or compensation.

The public-resource dimension of the public-trust conception of property includes but goes beyond the avoidance of harm rationale. It recognizes the role of private property in progress and that it increases our ability to discharge our natural-law duties. So it is quite natural on this conception that we set limits on the extent and characteristics of the way people's use of their property effects others. And that we go beyond this to use the benefits of private property for the benefit of all. The United States' Constitution straddles the forbearance and public-benefit dimensions of the public-trust conception in allowing taxation for the 'common defense and the general welfare.'[10] On this view stopping at the forbearance interpretation of the public-trust version constitutes theft because it does not allow the sharing of the fruits of private property, for example, through taxation. United States' Supreme Court decisions concerning property rights all exist within the policy space described by the two elements of the public-trust conception.[11]

PRIVATE PROPERTY IN THE COMMONWEALTH OF LIFE

Private property in the commonwealth of life (what I will call the fiduciary conception of property-rights) builds on the public-trust conception but carries it one step further. It recognizes rights and duties of property owners to other persons but places these rights and duties alongside our obligations to other species. It makes explicit the interpenetrating character of human actions on each other and on other species. It recognizes persons as members of the commonwealth of life not as masters of it. Of the three schools considered it is the only conception of property rights compatible with the findings of modern physics in that it emphasizes the interpenetrating character of actions at the molecular level. It is the only version that is compatible with the revisions of the human place in the universe required by Darwinian biology. It rests on the ethical principles set out in Chapter 2. It has a radical implication: it rejects the transformative value conception as a complete account of the legitimate origins of private property. It explicitly states that there is property that should *not* be transformed. It has found legal embodiment in the United States Endangered Species Act, and the UN Convention on Biodiversity.

OBJECTIONS

There are a number of objections to the idea of private property in the commonwealth of life. First, it could be argued that it is confiscatory; that it takes away, or at least substantially reduces, the rights of the owners of property to do as they wish with their property. Second, it could be held to be infeasible, to be so far outside the present humans-only conception of property rights that it is politically unpalatable. Third, it will be argued that it would result in a substantial reduction in value of people's existing holdings.

CONFISCATION

The perspective of the commonwealth of life helps us to reframe the issue of what is confiscatory. It is the transformative value framework that lies beneath current conceptions of private-property rights that is confiscatory. It takes as its mandate, carried to its logical conclusion, alteration of the conditions for all of the life on the earth. It has legitimated a massive taking of life and livelihood across much of our planet. We need to give a new and expanded sense to Locke's phrase that taking from the commons must leave 'enough and as good' for others, but in this case the 'others' is the commonwealth of life. Of course, living at all requires the taking of some life, even for vegetarians. So the objective cannot reasonably be formulated as doing nothing to kill or even impair the livelihood of other organisms. But the present regime, at least as exhibited in micro- and macro-economics, offers no account at all of direct duties to organisms other than humans. As marginalists they are perfectly willing to calculate the monetary value of the remaining species as others are eliminated. The fiduciary conception charts a middle course between not living at all and extinguishing, or threatening to extinguish, millions of life forms other than our own. It says that there are limits to our rights to appropriate from the earth and its resources.

FEASIBILITY

Let's look at its effect of the fiduciary conception on each of the three characteristics of property rights: exclusion, use, and disposition. There is nothing in this conception that would rule out exclusion of other persons. However, the public-benefit feature of private property would suggest that benefits could include some use rights for the public. A system of designated countryside trails such as is the case in the United Kingdom is a preferable option to complete exclusion, especially in cases where property is concentrated in a few hands. The implementation of such a system should be as comprehensive as possible to avoid having heavy use for some landowners and none for others.

Nor would the fiduciary conception radically alter what property *use* rights really are. The notion that people may do whatever they wish with their property is an anarchical fantasy. The right to use property is already limited by the effect of that use on the property of others. Under the United States' Constitution, for example, the use of property may be restricted by the several states to protect and promote public health and safety. The fiduciary perspective simply expands the idea of whose health and safety is relevant. Rights of disposition would be unaffected; though, of course, similar restrictions on use would apply to the new as to the previous owner.

COST AND COMPENSATION

The fiduciary conception would result, no doubt, in additional uncompensated restrictions on the use of property to protect the workings of ecosystems, aquifers, control erosion, and so on. But no compensation is morally required since, once we recognize ourselves as members of the commonwealth of life and not its owners, there was no right to these uses to begin with. Even under existing United States' Supreme Court doctrine no compensation would be required unless all economic uses were prohibited. In these cases compensation should be paid on the same terms as it would be paid with the public-trust framework. Of course, where land is already in public ownership such considerations do not apply. In the numerous nations of the world without private-property systems, it would be advisable to start with the fiduciary conception to begin with. As expectations of use settle around these norms, issues of compensation would not arise. The characteristics of property rights would depend on the kind of information gathered pursuant to the recommendations in part one of Chapter 7.

118

NOTES

1. Paul Wapner, 'Governance in Global Civil Society' in *Global Governance*, p. 72.
2. Milton Friedman, *Capitalism and Freedom*.
3. Garrett Hardin, 'The Tragedy of the Commons,' *Science* 162 (1968): pp. 1243–8
4. Anderson and Leal, *Free Market Environmentalism*, and Joseph Henry Vogel, *Genes for Sale: Privatization as a Conservation Policy*. My discussion of the short comings of bureaucracy on pp. 109–10 also draws on Anderson and Leal.
5. William Cronon, *Changes in the Land: Indians, Colonists, and the Ecology of New England*.
6. Joseph L. Sax, 'Legal and Policy Challenges of Environmental Restoration,' a paper presented at 'Wolves and Human Communities: Biology, Politics and Ethics,' American Museum of Natural History, New York, 21–23 October 1998.
7. Elinor Ostrom, *Governing the Commons*, p. 30.
8. Robert Nozick, *Anarchy, State and Utopia*, p. 177.
9. John Locke, *Second Treatise*, para. 32.
10. US Constitution, Art. 1, #8, cl. 1.
11. Joseph L. Sax, 'Property Rights in the US Supreme Court: A Status Report,' *Journal of Environmental Law*, vol. 7, no. 139, 1988, pp. 139–54.

PART III
TRANSPARENT
SOVEREIGNTY

INTRODUCTION

Part Three argues that the conduct of nations should be open to international scrutiny concerning human rights and the commonwealth of life. It concludes with a new vision of the relations among nations.

Chapter 6, 'Global Ethics and Fiduciary States,' argues in favor of a fiduciary conception of international relations. It shows that the ways we think about the relations between nations are confused. Realism, the idea that each state should pursue its own legitimate interests, is an illusion without coherent norms or empirical support. The idea of autonomous states, that each state has a domain of privacy beyond the proper reach of other states, rests on a misleading metaphor. The trading states model that lies behind economic neo-liberalism makes assumptions about economics, human well-being, and the natural world that are untenable. Humanitarianism is an important ally of the fiduciary conception defended here. It represents a partial step in the right direction.

Chapter 7, 'The Nation and the World' is organized into two parts. The first covers the characteristics of a well-ordered nation. These characteristics include protecting the three basic rights; efficient use of resources; improved indicators of economic and other performance; tax policy; land-use policy, including inventories of and protection for biodiversity, farmland, forests, and wetlands; population limitation; legal standing for other species and for future generations; rights of collective bargaining; education, and directions for scientific research.

The second part builds on these ideas to construct a model of transparent relations among trustee states. This model includes co-operative foreign policy to keep and/or restore peace and secure human rights; global institution building for resource and ecosystem protection; accountable global markets; redirected international lending practices, and so on. I conclude with a new vision of international relations in which realism, personal (as opposed to state) autonomy, and humanitarianism all play subordinate roles within an overall framework of the commonwealth of life.

CHAPTER 6

GLOBAL ETHICS AND
FIDUCIARY STATES

You should not destroy what is our common protection, the privilege of being
allowed in danger to evoke what is fair and right.

(Thucydides, *History of the Peloponnesian War*)

We turn here to transparent sovereignty in the commonwealth of life: to
developing the implications of the fiduciary perspective for the relations
between nations. It depicts the world as *a community of fiduciary states*,
with economic institutions designed to support stewardship, and with robust
civil societies in support of human rights and the commonwealth of life.
After the elements of this model are set out it is contrasted with four others:
realism, the autonomy of states, the trading states model, and a close cognate
to the fiduciary conception: humanitarianism. Unprioritized elements of
these four schools of thought make up our present *ad hoc* conception of
the relations between nations. To bring order to the relations between
nations we need to build or discover a foundational framework within
which these others will fit. Without such a framework we can only
anticipate a continuance of the disorder and destruction that characterizes
our times. The chapter concludes with a defense of the fiduciary model.

A COMMUNITY OF FIDUCIARY STATES

Nowhere does Locke limit the scope of obligations to compatriots. He
talks of our obligation to preserve all humankind, and this obligation
creates a transboundary frame of reference for evaluating the conduct of
nations. It is therefore a cosmopolitan theory of morality in which each
person is a global citizen. As Nigel Dower puts it in *World Ethics: The
New Agenda*:

> To be a global citizen ... is first to accept ... that one has duties in principle
> towards anyone in the world; second, to believe that there are a range of ways in
> which individuals can act so as to make a difference ... in the world; third, to
> engage ... in patterns of action which one would not have engaged in but for this
> belief.[1]

123

The conception of the global citizen simply applies the golden rule across space. A Lockean model of international relations is triple layered. First, persons have natural-law obligations to respect the natural rights of others. Second, because of the 'inconveniences of the state of nature' governments are necessary to ensure that people discharge these obligations. Governments act, or must be prepared to act, in a default capacity to protect the rights of their citizens. Third, both governments and citizens alike have obligations beyond their own borders; for Locke's account is about *human* rights, not only about the rights of those who share our nationality. Individuals have reciprocal duties to respect each other's rights wherever they may be; governments have reciprocal duties to other governments to see that their fiduciary duties are discharged to their own citizens. This is how Locke grounds a global world ethic.

Most contemporary theories of the state provide no account of what we owe to noncompatriots, persons who live outside of our borders.[2] But this cannot be satisfactory for two reasons. First, while theories of the nation state assume that duties of justice stop at national borders, most accounts of morality refer to duties to all persons. Second, as the world gets more and more interconnected through the environment, communication, and trade, there is even less reason than there ever was to believe that the effects of our actions stop at the border. Of course, a government's primary duties are to its own citizens. But duties to the citizens of other nations are default obligations that must be discharged if a state is failing to protect those rights itself. The state that intervenes to bring civil order in a conflict in another country acts to discharge the (natural-law) obligations of its own citizens.

Of course, my account of transboundary obligations is broader than Locke's would have been if he had drawn the international implications of his theory. This is because Locke limited his account of obligation to persons. I have expanded the conception of duties that apply within a Lockean framework by including consideration of the commonwealth of life. The general shape of these international default duties can then be derived from what the state minimally owes its own citizens. *Here, then, are the requirements of transparent sovereignty:* to protect the basic rights of its citizens; to act impartially; to derive its legitimacy from the consent of the governed; to avoid waste; to protect and restore the commonwealth of life; and to enable its citizens to achieve wealth within the legitimate range depicted by the fiduciary perspective. These are the minimal requirements that each state, and each global citizen, must respect. These are minimal not discretionary duties that we should require of ourselves and of all others.

CONTRASTS

In our era the relations between nations are described in four frameworks. Each framework carries with it prescriptive norms about behavior which have important, even life and death implications, for our fellow humans and often irreversible consequences for the commonwealth of life at large. Most of us subscribe to more than one of them. Each of these points of view captures dimensions of what we think and feel about the relations between nations and what the citizens of one nation owe to those of another. In some cases they also capture something of our attitude toward nature. The question is which framework, which set of terms of discourse are primary, which secondary, and which tertiary.

Here are the four discourses with which we are working. First, foreign policy realism: the idea that the goal of foreign policy should be to advance the interests of citizens, most especially their protection from each other and from assault by members of other groups. This position is usually combined with the proviso that the pursuit of interests should be limited to the degree that it comes into conflict with the legitimate interests of other states.

A second is the autonomy of states: states have a domain of internal or domestic affairs that others, usually other states, may not justly interfere with. According to this school of thought states have privacy rights just as individuals do. States may do as they wish with respect to their citizens and their environment.

Third, there is the school of thought, that is now becoming the most dominant: the regime of trading states. This point of view emphasizes that it is appropriate for states to pursue the economic interests of their own citizens through trade, while at the same time claiming that the benefits of trade accrue to all who participate. It thus draws together, and derives moral authority from, elements of the realist school and those of humanitarianism. Interestingly, from the point of view of the core argument of this book, it also breaches the wall of state autonomy by its requirement that actions be transparent with respect to state interferences with market forces such as subsidies or tariffs.

Fourth, there is the humanitarian strand that emphasizes that there are obligations to help those in other countries who are suffering from famine, earthquake and/or civil wars. For many, this school of thought derives its authority from the teachings of several of the world's religions that there is an obligation to help the vulnerable. An increasingly important related school of thought emphasizes that nature itself is vulnerable and that there are legitimate transboundary concerns that the citizens of one country may have in the treatment of the environment in other countries. Witness global concerns about tropical and temperate rainforest alike.

REALISM

To the realist the world is a tough place. Humans are prone to attack one another. They murder, assault, rape, and steal from one another. One of the primary rationales for the creation of the nation state to begin with is to protect the citizens from this behavior on the part of others. This rationale underlies the theories of Hobbes, Locke, and our contemporary Robert Nozick. It gains considerable support from socio-biology, which emphasizes the way in which evolution selects for aggression and sometimes violence.[3] It is the chief function of the state to protect us from each other.

Realism as a way of thinking about the relations between nations simply ramps up from this picture of behavior between individuals. At the national and international level realism is grounded in a picture of the world that says, in effect, that if each nation does not pursue its interests it will be overrun by, or become the pawn of, other nations. Fight, or at least be prepared to fight, or die. Put this way the rights of states are grounded in the rights of individuals to protect themselves, a right denied by few. They are 'realists' in seeing the world not as it ought to be, but for what it is. They are skeptical that moral rules can or will evolve that will govern the relations among nations. Foreign policy should seek to promote the interests of the citizens in a variety of forms. The prevention of invasion, the expansion of the territory or at least the economy, and the cultivation and preservation of the institutions of the nation are the primary objectives of the foreign policy process.

As Charles Beitz has pointed out in his *Political Theory and International Relations* there are a number of elements in the realist point of view.[4]

1. The actors in international relations are states. If there are significant other actors they could serve to mitigate, direct or even eliminate the interstate conflict predicted by the realists' account.
2. There are no enforceable international norms. The lack of enforceable norms means that there is no dependable world order to which states must subordinate themselves. Nor given the heterogeneous nature of the world community are such norms likely to evolve.
3. States are able to control their internal affairs independently of each other.
4. There is no dominant power. If there was a state that dominated the rest it could enforce its will anywhere in the world, and the war of all against all that lies at the heart of the realists' picture of the world would not be present.

There are two sorts of problems with this picture: empirical and conceptual.

Empirical Problems

It is evident that each of the four assumptions of the realist account is false. First, there are numerous other actors on the world stage besides sovereign states. These include the United Nations, the World Bank, numerous charitable organizations, international monitoring groups such as Amnesty International, the International Union for the Conservation of Nature, and so on. Nor is the second assumption correct. The realists' prediction that at least some basic, enforceable international norms will not evolve is implausible. Large ethnically diverse states such as the United States, Canada, India and others show that common norms can develop and be adhered to by persons from extremely diverse backgrounds over very large geographical space. What has happened within nations not only can but has happened between them. There are many thousands of international treaties, most of which are complied with most of the time.[5] There are numerous enforcement mechanisms for bringing about compliance. These range from symbolic actions such as banning from international athletic events, trade sanctions, embargoes, the threat of, and the use of, military force on the part of the international community.

Third, nor are states able to set their policies independently of each other. Interdependence has increased substantially in economic policy since interest rates and other economic effects have substantial effects in other countries.[6] Air and water pollution cross national boundaries and are increasingly regulated under international treaties; the framework for an international treaty on climate has been developed. Fourth, there are dominant regional and international powers, most notably the United States and its affiliates such as the North Atlantic Treaty Organization, which can impose their will on weaker nations thus further undermining the validity of the metaphor of the war of all against all.

Most telling perhaps is the fact that realism is not realistic. It abstracts from all of human behavior emphasizing those elements that lead to violence and the narrow pursuit of interests. Of course, these elements are facts of the human condition. But they are only strands, albeit significant ones in a broader and much more complex fabric. For all the fanfare that attaches to a Machiavellian account of the actions of men, it is Aristotle that offers the more empirically correct account of human behavior: as human beings, as members of communities, as capable of seeking and achieving balance, as susceptible to moral education and responsible action.[7]

Conceptual Problems

But beyond these empirical difficulties there are conceptual ones as well. Realism falls into self-contradiction at the outset as a guide to action. It claims to be nonmoral, just a description of the way the world works. But it necessarily asserts a normative standard: that states *ought* to pursue their interests. There are three difficulties here connected to the relation between morality and national interests. First, it is implausible to rest a normative system solely on the pursuit of interests.[8] Any *moral* system requires some limitation on interests; indeed, a way to characterize moral systems is by the way they restrict the pursuit of interests. To be moral a system of thought must say which interests are legitimate and which are not. Second, realists also fail to explain why the pursuit of *interests* is legitimate. Realism is grounded in the idea of self-preservation, a widely recognized right at least since the eighteenth century. But the concept of interests is broader than the concept of survival. I may have interests in wealth, art, or leisure, but the satisfaction of these interests surely has less force than my own self-preservation. Hence, the national *interest* standard, broadly construed, goes beyond this right of self-defense, so the moral grounding offered is insufficient. Third, it is hard to see why the interests to be pursued are *national*, unless this is taken to be a shorthand for the interests of the individuals who make up the nation in question. Individuals have interests in survival, pleasure, property, their families and the like.[9] But states are not like persons. When the state owns property, say a national forest, there is no one who owns it as there is when we say a person owns his or her house. It is the citizens of the nation that own the forest, and they form certain expectations – many of them codified in law about how the resource is to be used. The realist may reply that 'the *national* interest' is a summary expression for the common interests of the citizens. But the common interests of the citizens are likely to be limited to certain basic things like survival, and as we go further beyond this unanimity is harder and harder to find.

This ambiguity in the scope of its concepts leads to a second class of difficulties with realism. Few really believe in realism or the attendant national interest standard in its most simple form. Even the most ardent proponents usually qualify their arguments by pointing out that states should pursue their *legitimate* interests. But the word 'legitimate' is left undefined. This leaves the real work about what we should do all undone. The best face that can be put on realism is that it is a device to oppose naive moralism in foreign policy,[10] but absent in it is a moral foundation for thinking about the relations between states. Realism does not offer a means of discussing what to do.

But the absence of guidance about what to do is not the worst of it. Realism pushes behavior toward the least common denominator. The realist's assessment of the world legitimates the pursuit of self-interest, then the realist turns around and says 'I told you so.' Realists brand as unrealistic those who seek on the individual or institutional level to point in a more balanced and constructive direction. It diverts attention from the construction of institutions which can redirect the energies that lie behind the behaviors at the core of the realist's unrealistic vision.

THE AUTONOMY OF STATES

One response to realism's inability to offer constructive guidance on what to do is to repair to a different vocabulary, an alternative frame of reference. Perhaps the second most prominent framework is that of the autonomy of states. Like realism this school of thought ramps up from characteristics of individuals to characteristics of groups. Just as persons have privacy rights so do states. The essential features of this school boil down to four elements as summarized by Dower:[11]

1. 'The preservation of the state and the system of states itself.' Each state tries to preserve itself and to observe rules that will lead to the stability of states. This leads to various practices designed to facilitate communication, protect diplomats, and make international relations run smoothly. States have duties to honor their agreements.

2. 'The maintenance of the independence and external sovereignty of individual states.' Each state is autonomous and directs its own internal affairs. One state should not interfere in the 'domestic' affairs of another. States offer this as a defense against an undesired intervention on the grounds that there are certain things that should be left for the people and/or the government to decide. These include how to handle civil wars, the management of their criminal justice system, the treatment of natural and cultural resources, and the like.

3. 'The maintenance and pursuit of peace.' The goal of the preservation of states and the system of states can be pursued by seeking peace, even though states may acquire and use armed force in pursuit of this objective. The general duty to promote peace may be overridden in special circumstances, but the conduct of war must be subordinate to internationally agreed upon norms in the manner it is conducted.

4. 'The common goals of social life.' The existence of the system of states is justified by reference to the security of a set of commonly accepted values. These may be specified in a variety of ways. Whatever claims individuals have against governments in support of these goals can only properly be made against their own government.

This framework of discourse is also unsatisfactory for at least three reasons. First, the autonomy of states vocabulary fails because the analogy with persons is inappropriate.[12] States do not have bodies or memories as persons do. States are made up of persons who have privacy rights, but the state itself has no such rights. If we are really concerned with autonomy and privacy we have to be concerned with these things for individuals, and not for states. Thus the whole argument may backfire since protecting the autonomy of persons could legitimate substantial interventions with the behavior of states with respect to the treatment of their citizens. For example, if a state is torturing its own citizens, intervention could be justified to preserve the autonomy of the person. However, from the point of view of the autonomy of states, this would be an interference with a domestic matter.

Second, the boundaries of what is a domestic concern only, and what is also of legitimate international concern is left unspecified. Standard four above can often conflict with standard two. If there are universally shared values then it is not clear why it is only the duty of the state of which I am a citizen to protect them. Not all states have the means, or the inclination, to discharge all their obligations to their citizens. In cases of famine, natural disaster, or severe corruption a state may not be able to protect its own citizens thus requiring help from the international community. The state independence standard thus begs the central question: how far may, and how far must, the citizens of one state take into account the well-being and actions of the citizens of another state? Like realism, it leaves the central question unanalyzed. Yet, like realism the autonomy of states viewpoint captures something that we think is true about states and their relations to each other, but remains *ad hoc* without a wider institutional and moral context.

Third, many concerns, especially environmental ones, may overlap state boundaries. The state of the Great Lakes are of valid concern to both the United States and Canada. Climate change is a legitimate concern to all persons and all states. Once the international community begins to insert itself into the energy-use practices of the world's nations, vast areas of allegedly domestic concern will fall under the scrutiny of the world community.

TRADING STATES

The trading-states model ramps the insights about how individuals gain from trade, set out in Chapter 3 to the level of the nation state. If individuals always gain from exchange so will nations.[13] This is called the theory of comparative advantage, an idea first systemically advanced by David Ricardo.[14] Each nation produces what it can make most efficiently and sells it to other nations in exchange for what the other nations produce most efficiently. Capitalists will seek the highest rate of return in their own country. Goods made in the home country that it can produce best (compared to other domestically produced goods) can be sold to other countries which are pursuing their own comparative advantage. Say country A can produce two goods, wine and cheese, but can produce wine more efficiently than cheese relative to country B, which, in this comparison, can produce cheese more efficiently than wine. Each country will benefit by producing what it can do more efficiently and trading that good with the other country. Thus by concentrating on producing wine country A will be able to consume more *cheese* than it could if it tried to produce cheese on its own. Thus, so the theory goes, every country gains which participates in trade. Accordingly, all nations benefit. The prospect of a prosperous world appears happily on the horizon. To assure that nations do not try to gain unfair advantage by aiding or protecting certain industries this model requires that their actions be open to inspection by other nations. This is the economists' view of the idea of transparent sovereignty.

The problem is made more complicated by three factors when contrasted to trade between individuals within a nation. First, there is the matter of the relative value of different currencies. We need some sort of international standard by which to compare the value of various currencies so we can calculate the value of goods in various countries. The gold standard served this purpose for a while, now it is the dollar, it may be something else in the future. But the fundamental insight that all nations who engage in the transaction benefits appears to remain intact.

The second way that international trade is different from that within a nation is that nations have the power to restrict what is imported in ways that they do not customarily have with respect to trade within their borders. They may, for example, restrict or place tariffs on textiles to protect the domestic industry. Trade theorists typically oppose such *protectionist* measures on the grounds that they are efficiency reducing. This is so because a country's economy will not function optimally since resources are devoted to the production of goods that do not reflect its highest comparative advantage. Purchasers of goods in the protecting country pay more for textiles than they otherwise would, cut back on the purchase of other goods, and hence enjoy a lower level of economic well-being than would otherwise be the case. Protectionism is thus wasteful.[15]

The third contrast relates to the relative immobility of labor. In a domestic economy workers may move from one location to another to respond to employment opportunities, though often with considerable disruption in their personal lives. But labor mobility is sharply, but by no means completely, restricted between countries. Proponents of the trading-states model are normally split on the question of whether or not there should be complete labor mobility across borders.

There are a number of moral arguments in favor of world trade. Each nation can claim to advance the interests of its citizens by facilitating opportunities for voluntary exchange. It can reduce poverty by expanding global economic activity and including more and more of the world's poor and near poor in productive work with adequate recompense. It seems to leave each state free to pursue its own interests, with the exception that each state must do nothing to interfere with the proper operation of efficient markets.

There are a number of reasons for thinking that we should not accept the trading-states model as foundational in our thinking about international relations. In part this is simply because it cannot satisfactorily answer, or to some extent does not even recognize, the six questions set out in Chapter 3: what is the economy for; how does, and how should it, fit in the world's biophysical systems; how much economic growth is enough; should we judge the processes of industrial production; how should we think about the future, and what institutional structure does the market economy assume? This is not to say, of course, that there should not be an international economics; but only that we should not entrust such an ill-thought through regime to protect human rights and/or protect and restore the commonwealth of life.

It is the failure to pay attention to the background institutions that further plague the international version of the neo-classical regime. These relate to both its account of the relations between nations and within nations.

Intra-national Institutional Shortcomings
The world-trade regime sets up incentives for countries to fail to internalize costs in order to remain competitive in world markets. It has an inadequate conception of a subsidy. By offering products in world markets for less their full market price countries can beat out competitors in getting a share of world trade. It allows the poor to subsidize markets with their lungs, and forests to subsidize them with their topsoil. There are no penalties for countries which fail to internalize prices. Thus, as partial as the goal of efficiency may be neo-classical economics is incapable – due to inattention to its own institutional context – of delivering on its own object.

International Problems with the Trading-States Model
But the problem is even broader than this. It is not only the fact that many nations lack the institutions necessary for the operation of efficient markets. These institutions do not exist in the space between nations either. Take the case of antitrust: the ability to break up concentrations of economic power to assure that competitive markets operate. For efficient markets to function there would have to be ways to prevent or break up monopolies of institutions that exist *between* nations, such as shipping capabilities like container ports, or financial institutions that own large amount of assets in various parts of the world. Most such international institutions which are necessary for the operation of efficient markets do not exist.

But the problems do not stop here. As we have just seen economists typically assert that we know from the theory of comparative advantage that free trade will benefit all nations which participate. It cannot be emphasized enough that trade theory which increasingly dominates the world is empirically false. Ricardo's theory depends on the *immobility* of capital (and labor and raw materials) across national boundaries, but the assumption regarding capital mobility is not even remotely approximated in the world today. This undercuts the central claim of the free-trade theory: that free trade benefits all *nations* which participate. With the international mobility of capital there is no reason to think that capital will seek its highest comparative advantage in its own country, but rather will seek its highest *absolute* advantage anywhere in the world. The difference between comparative and absolute advantage changes everything.

There is no reason to think that *all* countries which participate in trade will achieve their comparative advantage because the necessary capital will have moved somewhere else in the world seeking the highest *absolute* rate of return. Thus, an industrial country such as the United States, which participates in free-trade arrangements such as World Trade Organization and North American Free Trade Agreement, may *not* be a net beneficiary. Which nations benefit and which ones lose has to be determined empirically in the world of absolute advantage. In contrast, being a beneficiary follows deductively in the comparative advantage model. Poor countries rather than using their scarce available capital to derive the most of their comparative advantage will often see that capital migrate to another part of the globe seeking its *absolute* advantage.[16]

HUMANITARIANISM

Humanitarian concerns are often grounded in religious beliefs concerning the sanctity of human life, or in secular accounts that emphasize the equality of persons. Assistance to persons in other nations is typically justified by reference to two interrelated conceptions. One is the duty to protect the vulnerable,[17] the other is grounded in ideas of universal human rights that all persons share, and that others have direct or indirect duties to protect. Vulnerability-based humanitarian rationales typically underlie rescue efforts in the aftermath of disasters such as earthquakes, floods, or severe droughts. They are also elements in justifying long-term assistance for the improvement of agriculture, and family-planning assistance. Efforts to assist industrial and commercial development – a central feature of the trading-states model – find an element of their justification in efforts to alleviate poverty and thus protect people from its related scourges of malnutrition, disease, and the like.

The emerging, but still far from complete, global consensus about the fundamental nature of human rights is an important strand in the humanitarian account of cross-boundary duties. There is still considerable dispute within this school of thought about what rights are to be protected. Bodily integrity rights, not to be tortured, murdered, raped, imprisoned without due process, and the like, have gained acceptance by many, if not most. More disputed are rights concerning moral, religious, and political choice, and whether there are attendant cross-boundary duties to promote and protect such rights. Consensus is weakest on the question of whether there are rights to subsistence, and if there are, who has the corresponding duties. For the purposes of the argument in favor of universal trusteeship this school of thought is an important ally because it breaches the wall of national borders, and opens the way for the development of an international consensus on how to treat our fellow persons, and – suitably expanded – the rest of the commonwealth of life.

The model of trustee states brings order to a cacophony of voices concerning international relations. It provides a way of encompassing and ranking these various realms of discourse. We saw that the national-interest standard, which is the core of realism, failed to provide an adequate framework for discussing the relationships between nations, in part, because it left the concept of what was 'legitimate' unanalyzed. By specifying the functions of governments the fiduciary conception fills in what governments owe their own citizens, and those abroad; and to the commonwealth of life. Once these duties within and beyond borders have been discharged governments are free to pursue the national interest as they see it. Similarly, these realms that are not part of fiduciary duties are properly referred to as domestic concerns and can be legitimately screened from those who are not citizens or residents. A global stewardship economics could flourish within the fiduciary framework while at the same time respecting human rights and the commonwealth of life.

DEFENDING THE FIDUCIARY CONCEPTION

There could be a number of objections to the fiduciary conception. One is that it weakens sovereignty, the other that it asks too much.

It is true that the fiduciary account limits sovereignty in ways that other models do not. But the system of sovereign states that emerged in enlightenment Europe is under pressure from within, often by those who question the very legitimacy of government at all. From without the trading-states scheme, the interpenetrating of markets, the mobility of capital and the emergence of a global, and among many an electronic, civil society alter the underlying model of the sovereign state. The fiduciary account of transparent sovereignty focuses attention on another set of interrelations: the underlying unity of humanity, and the common heritage and destiny we share with the rest of life.

In *Why Sovereignty Matters* Jeremy Rabkin worries that international treaties to control greenhouse gas emissions are threats to sovereignty.

His worries are threefold. First, that decision-making power will be delegated to bodies unaccountable to the United States constitutional system. Because of the complexity of the decisions not all the details will be available in the treaty itself. As a consequence 'a single act of ratification would seem to be committing the United States to a vast amount of subsequent policy decision by foreigners.'[18] Second, that the effects of climate change are 'remote and tenuous.'[19] Third, that the treaty is not reciprocal; that it commits the United States to emission reductions while not requiring the same of other nations.

Each of these points needs answering. First, there is nothing in the idea of transparent sovereignty that would allow us to substitute openness about what nations are doing for closedness by international decision-making bodies. All deliberations that affect the international community must be open to all. The issue of whether someone is a foreigner or not is irrelevant. What matters is whether they are operating fairly and openly in regard to previously agreed and specified standards. Second, it is true that the effects of emissions are remote. Driving a car in Kansas will affect weather in remote time and places. But the effects are not tenuous. There is a widespread agreement that carbon-dioxide concentrations in the atmosphere are rising, and a virtual consensus that climate change is already underway. Third, Rabkin is right about reciprocity, but the idea needs to be specified much more carefully than he does. In the long term nations should not agree to be bound by agreements that do not bind other similarly situated nations. But as the country that produces over 20 per cent of emissions with about 6 per cent of the world's population the United States is not similarly situated with respect to other nations. It is true that, in the long run, climate stabilization will require the contribution of all, and so eventually all nations will have to be part of a treaty agreement. But given its record it is a duty of the United States to set an example for a period of time while trying to bring all nations within an emissions control system.

Nevertheless, the obligation to preserve all persons, and to respect and enhance the commonwealth of life, might seem especially demanding and disruptive once we recognize its global implications. It might seem to require too much. The underlying global duty of respecting rights and the commonwealth of life is first of all an obligation of citizens. At times our individual obligations are properly discharged indirectly through the governments of the world – the community of trustees.[20] The citizens of one nation have duties beyond borders only when the other government does not or cannot discharge its duties. Trustees do have the conventional duties of aid in times when local resources are overwhelmed by natural disaster, civil strife and the like, but their primary international duty is to

136

work for a just world order where the rights of persons around the globe are satisfied by their own governments, and the commonwealth of life secure. Except for responding to natural disasters, in a just and well-ordered world we could legitimately attend only to compatriots and the commonwealth of life within our own borders.

NOTES

1. Nigel Dower, *World Ethics: The New Agenda*, p. 107. This volume contains an excellent account of the various schools of thought about international relations, and favors a cosmopolitan ethic similar in the main to that defended in many ways in this book.
2. See, for example, John Rawls, *A Theory of Justice*, and Robert Nozick, *Anarchy, State and Utopia*.
3. Konrad Lorenz, *On Aggression* and Richard Wrangham and Dale Peterson, *Demonic Males*.
4. This account of realism and its shortcomings draws on Charles Beitz, *Political Theory and International Relations*, pp. 15–66.
5. Raymond L. Bridgman in *The First Book of Law* identifies nineteen international conventions or treaties, covering the areas of the postal union, arbitration, navigation, disarmament, the common prime meridian, the sea, sanitation, industrial property, submarine cables, slave trade, trade in white women, agriculture, the Red Cross, weights and measures, wireless telegraphy, exchange of documents, the world judiciary, the world executive, and peace and good will.
6. For a discussion of the way the interdependence of nations undercuts realism see Robert O. Keohane, and Joseph S. Nye, *Power and Interdependence: World Politics in Transition*. Like much of the post-war literature on international relations these authors, still largely operating within the confines of positivism, shy away from offering explicit normative arguments about how international relations should be structured. This, in turn, has a tendency to ratify the status quo since it offers no critique of it. Dower makes these points on p. 8 of *Global Ethics*.
7. Robert K. Faulkner, *Francis Bacon and the Project of Progress*.
8. Beitz, *Political Theory and International Relations*.
9. Max Weber, *The City*.
10. Arthur Schlessinger, Jr 'National Interests and Moral Absolutes' in E. LeFever (ed.), *Ethics and World Politics: Four Perspectives*.
11. Here I follow Dower, *Global Ethics*, pp. 52–5.
12. Beitz, *Political Theory and International Relations*.
13. Paul R. Krugman and Maurice Obstfeld, *International Economics: Theory and Policy*.
14. David Ricardo, *Principles of Political Economy and Taxation*, Sraffa Edition.
15. Anne O. Krueger, 'Free Trade is the Best Policy' in Robert Z. Lawrence and

Charles Schultze (eds), *An American Trade Strategy: Options for the 1990s*.

16. Nor do other theories of international trade help with this dilemma. For example, the Heckscher-Ohlin theory of trade emphasizes the role of different resource endowments in explaining comparative advantage. Other models emphasize different factors or combinations of factors. These other theories do *nothing at all* to address the point in question since they too assume that capital, at least largely, remains in its home country. Present arrangements allow the owners of capital to appropriate otherwise unclaimed environmental services, and exploit unprotected labor, leading to a standards-lowering competition that achieves cheapness by simply not counting costs. Some countries have adopted policies of maintaining comparative advantage by specializing in activities that other countries are not willing to do, or at least to admit they are doing it: specializing in the sale of sex, for example, as in the case of Thailand.

17. Robert E. Goodin, *Protecting the Vulnerable: A Reanalysis of Our Social Responsibilities*.

18. Jeremy Rabkin, *Why Sovereignty Matters*, p. 82.

19. Ibid., p. 82.

20. This is far preferable to the onerous duties in classical utilitarianism that makes us responsible for the *happiness* of all persons – far too strong a set of obligations to make it possible to preserve our own purposes and project. It is thus incompatible with a moral and religious life. This is brilliantly argued by Bernard Williams in his 'Critique of Utilitarianism,' in Smart and Williams, *Utilitarianism For and Against*. It is also preferable to the account of Friedman which says that we have *no* obligations to others, thus having an ethic that flies in the face of the fundamentals of the Judeo-Christian tradition. Welfare economics is still stuck with the principle of utility in principle along with its too strong a requirement of altruism, but dodges it in practice with the idea of the invisible hand and by not having any principle of distribution. The trustee doctrine steers a nice middle course between these two implausible accounts of our duties to noncompatriots.

CHAPTER 7

THE NATION AND THE WORLD

Sooner or later there must dawn the true and final Renaissance which will bring peace to the world

(Albert Schweitzer, *The Philosophy of Civilization*)

We are at a largely unrecognized turning point. The globalization of the world economy, without the development of global institutions, has established trends that erode the ability of nations to discharge their traditional functions. These include the ability of nations to provide for income (or subsistence) security, and environmental protection. As we have seen, since the apparent costs of production will be cheaper elsewhere nations that undertake to discharge these functions will be increasing noncompetitive in a world of mobile capital seeking its absolute advantage. The present scheme that alleges to aim at perfectly functioning markets rewards nations that fail to impose the very conditions that properly functioning markets require.

Constructing a world dedicated to human rights and the commonwealth of life will require strong governments subject to fiduciary international standards. Nations will need to adopt policies that allow them to set their own standards in discharging their traditional functions. These are discussed in detail under the section 'Trade' in this chapter (see pp. 155–6). This chapter first sets out what each nation should do in terms of its domestic policy, and then offers an account of international obligations and institutions consistent with our obligations to the commonwealth of life. It thus draws the policy implications of the argument made so far in this book with particular emphasis on the actions that must be taken in light of duties to respect the commonwealth of life.

THE NATION

There are a number of institutions that need to be developed or altered, and a number of policies redirected within each nation. But, surprisingly, much is already underway in accomplishing this redirection; yet, to be

138

sure, these efforts are scattered and still subordinate to the growth model. What the fiduciary model does is to pull together, emphasize, and provide further impetus to existing nascent, scattered trends. Shifting from the present *ad hoc* arrangements to the stewardship model will require substantial redirection of efforts. In many nations substantial foreign assistance and/or revenues from international taxes will be required to accomplish the tasks that are described below.

In countries with functioning governments steps that should be taken to operationalize the duties of trusteeship include: an evaluation of its own citizenry with respect to the three basic rights; an assessment of its productive resources as a step in developing measures of growth efficiency; its share of an international biological survey to lay the ground work for an assessment of ecological efficiency; construction of institutions to protect the commonwealth of life: a redefinition and redirection of the role of the central banks; a restructuring of tax systems away from the taxing of income and toward taxing land and resource rents; the creation of a council of stewardship advisors to correspond to, or subsume the duties of, the councils of economic advisors; the creation of incentives for stewardship substitution; the granting of legal standing to future generations and other species; the development and implementation of cosmopolitan education; an international declaration of stewardship which would parallel and perhaps in part subsume the existing declaration of human rights; and the creation of an annual report of the world's trustees.

ASSESSING THE BASIC RIGHTS

Each government should assess the degree to which the three basic rights are protected for its own citizens. Given the human propensity toward violence perhaps the most basic precondition for securing basic rights is the establishment and maintenance of civil order. The balance of the policy prescriptions in this section assume the existence of this order, while the next section addresses the obligations of the international community in providing assistance to establish such an order.

GROWTH EFFICIENCY: INVENTORIES OF SOURCES AND SINKS

We need to inventory the world's productive resources: the ability to keep producing what we take from the resource. Each nation should assay the ability of various sinks to assimilate the byproducts of human activity. Internationally accepted standards need to be developed that would allow us to evaluate the size and characteristics of the world's forests, farmland, fisheries, wetlands, and aquifers. Each of these is currently undergoing very substantial degradation.

We need to know not only their current state, but also estimates of their capacity to rebound to various perturbations, and the margin of error for such estimates. For example, if we put pressure on a fishery how long will it take to rebound, and how much confidence can we have in such estimates? Many countries already have some such inventories, measures, and estimates; but they need to be standardized, pulled together, and undertaken where they are not done now. Of vital importance is not to frame these issues in terms of linear, as opposed to, co-evolutionary models. Particularly at the microbial and also at other levels evolution is continuing at a very rapid rate.[1] The world will not hold constant, waiting to rebound to a previous state of affairs.

Sinks of a variety of sources also need to be measured. We already know that we are unbalancing the ability of the atmosphere to recycle carbon dioxide and other heat-trapping gases. We need to assess the ability of the ocean to take up waste in addition to carbon dioxide; the ability of soils to neutralize pesticides; and the capacity of wetlands to process effluents. As the scale of human activity accelerates the need for these measurements will increase dramatically. Because of the international character of many, indeed most, of these major sinks the data should be collected in some standard, or some easily translated data forms. This will allow interpretations of trends and policies from a global perspective. For example, it would allow us to assess country by country carbon emissions into and withdrawals from the atmosphere, to understand the extent and character of wetland and farmland loss, and evaluate the sources and sinks of heavy metals such as lead and mercury.

ASSESSING ECOLOGICAL EFFICIENCY

Here we need to measure the ability of ecosystems to rebound from perturbations. A world biological survey, undertaken by individual nations using standardized techniques, is imperative. We already know that there is widespread species loss, but our knowledge about its scale and location varies widely. From a fiduciary perspective these losses are completely unacceptable. Yet in facing this issue we often focus, for example in the United States Endangered Species Act, on a very partial question: how to keep species from going extinct. We aim not to preserve the ragged remnants of the once magnificent loom of life, but to be part of a flourishing that cherishes what is left, and restores that which we can of what has been lost. Of course, much has been lost irretrievably. To assess the ways of increasing ecological efficiency we need to know what has been imperiled, and how these impacts can be eliminated, or at least mitigated. As in the case of growth efficiency we also need to know what can be restored, be cognizant of the widespread effects of ecological systems, and look at the co-evolutionary effects of past, present, and future policies. Without this knowledge it is impossible to measure the degree of ecological efficiency that can be achieved. Grants might be made to individual countries to undertake this work from the revenues generated by international taxes, as discussed in the section 'Institutional Design' below. Some of these monitoring functions would have to be sustained indefinitely.

INSTITUTIONAL DESIGN

Once these inventories of growth and ecological efficiency have been undertaken resource use should be constrained to preserve their capacities for the future. Fostering management systems for common-property resources such as described in Chapter 5 is a step in the right direction for many of the more local resources. There are a variety of reasons to want to retain, or alter only at the margin, existing arrangements between traditional human populations and the resources on which they depend. Forced resettlements of indigenous peoples in the name of development, privatization, and/or the restoration of wilderness is very often incompatible with the survival of these cultures. In addition, partly because it is hard to enforce, it often can result in degradation, rather than enhancement, of the resource base. Even adequately enforced complete removal of all people to establish a 'wilderness' area can backfire since it is often difficult to know in advance what new ecological equilibrium will follow. The idea that we can just let nature take its course may result in a simplification of the resources as was the case with Yellowstone National Park in the United States. There the elk herd, unconstrained by carnivorous predators such as wolves, which subsequently have been reintroduced, stripped much of the flora from the landscape resulting in substantial biological simplification, erosion and other undesirable consequences.[2]

Whether local institutions such as those described by Ostrom can be ramped up to deal with much larger resource preservation/management issues within and between nations, such as the North Atlantic Fisheries, the world's ozone layer, and the like, is an open question. My own assessment is that, in the absence of other more worked-out models, that this should be tried. Obviously, the number of people expands enormously, moving from several hundred to millions and tens of millions. But this can be dealt with by treating nations or other institutions such as corporations or interest-group representatives as individuals. For example, in achieving a reduction in ozone-depleting chemicals the parties at the bargaining table are not hundreds of millions of Chinese, but the government of China. Many of the other elements of the Ostrom model, such as verification of compliance with norms, and an external body capable of the enforcement of agreements, are essential. For reasons set out in Chapter 5 we should be very skeptical of 'magic bullet' solutions such as privatization, or highly centralized bureaucracies.

REGULATIONS AND INCENTIVES

We have seen above that one of the strengths of the fiduciary model is that it recognizes the difference between a harm and a wrong. These consider-ations are not part of the calculus offered by the cost-internalization model discussed in Chapter 3. Regulations are policies by which society states what it takes to be a wrong. It often accompanies these with severe, even criminal penalties. Certain prohibitions are central to the fiduciary model: with respect to persons practices that are at odds with autonomous persons in community should be severely sanctioned. In general these will be things that correspond to the three basic rights. Another class of prohibitions concerns the stewardship of the commonwealth of life: the filling of wetlands, the shooting of rare animals, the destruction of the habitat of rare plants are all common examples.

But much of what we need to accomplish is difficult to achieve using prohibitions. It is difficult to monitor compliance with a complex set of rules. Monitoring may interfere with the liberty of others. Regulations often do not allow people to find the least expensive way to achieve the policy objective. There may be activities that we wish to discourage, but where we may not wish, or may not be able to, prohibit the activity altogether. Cars have substantial deleterious effects, but in many 'advanced nations' it is difficult to see how they could be prohibited altogether. A well-ordered fiduciary state will hence have a set a regulations and a set of incentives. Regulations can be used to drive technological change in support of the twin goals of stewardship as the regulations governing automobile pollution in the United States hastened the development of cleaner cars. Incentives, as we shall see below, can also help to advance stewardship by shifting the composition of demand toward more efficient technologies; as efficiency is defined within the fiduciary model. These two instruments can thus work hand in hand.

A COUNCIL OF STEWARDSHIP ADVISORS

As the growth model is replaced by stewardship, governments will need to develop policies that move in the direction of satisfying the two principles. We need an institution parallel to, or as a replacement of, the Councils of Economic Advisors. Even the tentative list in this chapter shows that there are a number of policies that can be used to advance these objectives. There is every reason to believe that there are numerous others. These councils should be made up persons of diverse backgrounds, including physicians, ecologists, chemists, philosophers, and spiritual leaders from diverse faiths.

In the fiduciary model the role of the central banks shifts from the stimulation of growth with low inflation to a concern with all six efficiencies. These efficiencies define much of the policy space of the fiduciary model. The tools of fiscal and monetary policy are placed in service of the preservation of persons, and the commonwealth of life. This simply redirects or extends rationales already common that favor veterans in home and education loans, poor farmers, medical students, and so on. They can work hand in hand with regulations designed to promote service and maintenance efficiency by providing differential interest rates to companies exceeding the requirements set by regulation. Growth efficiency can be advanced by similar techniques. Loans can be refused altogether where a resource is already overused. One of the prime factors in the precipitous decline in the world fisheries was overcapitalization of fishing fleets. Differential loan rates can be set for farm machinery that conserves topsoil, or irrigation systems that use less water.

CHANGING OR EXPANDING THE INDICATORS

We need to take the criticisms of the GNP measure seriously and either eliminate it altogether as an indicator; or, at the very least, split it into a cost and benefit account. We already typically include employment. At a minimum nations that monitor their economic activity should couple their reports with data concerning human rights, and the preservation and enhancement of the commonwealth of life. For example, a list of a dozen or so indicators might be used which included GDP but which also reported on: the number of malnourished children, the number of disappeared girl babies, species lost or threatened, the percentage of the population in prison, the amounts of money representatives received to run for office, the number of acres of farmland lost, wetlands filled, tons of carbon dioxide emitted, and so on. This would give us a much better picture of our successes or failures than the current simple and misleading indicator(s). Countries that refuse to supply such information should be sanctioned along the lines set out in 'Creating Incentives for Stewardship Substitution' below. Of course, some of this information is already available from nongovernmental organizations. But there is considerable value in having the country itself supply the information as it would help to internalize these fiduciary norms.

TAX BADS NOT GOODS

In many, if not most, countries there is a tax on income, and frequently there are subsidies for resource extraction and use. This increases the cost of labor relative to natural resources and to capital generally. The fiduciary model is especially effective in calling attention to the fact that these arrangements are backwards. In a world where hundreds of millions lack gainful work, there are numerous reasons that we want more employment so that people can be self-supporting, have self-respect and the like. There are also the compelling reasons that emphasize the role of high levels of employment in social stability. Employment is something we want more of so let's lower its relative price.

Resource use is something we want less of because of its effect on future generations and on the commonwealth of life. So let's raise the relative prices of these practices. Paying attention to the four intermediate efficiencies helps us to see how to do this. Increasing the service efficiency of cars and appliances will, all things being equal, decrease pressure on resources and sinks alike. In addition to a regulatory structure that sets certain minimum standards of performance taxes can be used to shift the composition of demand in desired directions. For example, cars that are fuel inefficient can be taxed more than their more efficient counterparts, and the revenues used to reduce the cost of more efficient models. Examples of this sort abound. Similar considerations and policies also apply to maintenance efficiency.

Goods produced in ways that impair growth efficiency should be taxed differentially. Crops grown with techniques that waste topsoil, or logging practices that impede regrowth can be taxed in a different manner than others. Just as we already have ways of certifying that certain products are organic, or have come from forests managed in certain ways, so we can have a set of standards that reveals the growth efficiency of certain productive practices. Similar considerations obviously apply to ecological efficiency. Again, the tax structure would presuppose a regulatory framework. Goods and services that are produced in ways that create substantial collateral ecological damage could be taxed on a sliding scale. For example, many fishing techniques involve lots of 'by catch,' the practice of catching fish or other marine creatures other than those intended. In many cases the damage to nontarget species is considerable, even catastrophic. It should be remembered that in the fiduciary model we do not aim at some optimal level of damage as we do within the neo-classical model. Rather we seek the preservation and flourishing of the diversity of life itself.

It seems unlikely that ecological taxes will ever equitably supply all necessary revenues; though revenues from them could be rebated directly to the poor. The more effective they are in reducing demand for the taxed good the less revenue they yield, though once demand for the good becomes inelastic it can still be taxed. For this reason they are part of a portfolio of means, working hand and glove with regulation in achieving the objectives of stewardship. Some sort of progressive income taxes, coupled with income and other supplements to those in the lower ranges of the income distribution, are likely to be necessary. The mix, taking into account overall revenue needs, will obviously have to be empirically determined.

Taxes also serve to help promote the preservation and creation of autonomous persons. Taxes on cigarettes are now widely used to help discourage consumption of these addictive products. Similarly, tax rebates and other subsidies can be designed to lower the effective cost of education to consumers, and other elements in the creation of autonomous individuals.

CREATING INCENTIVES FOR STEWARDSHIP SUBSTITUTION
There are a number of ways to stimulate improvements in service, maintenance, growth, and ecological efficiency. Regulation is one instrument. They can simply prohibit the manufacture and sale of products that are at the low end of the efficiency spectrum. In the United States this is already done in the case of refrigerators with respect to service efficiency. It is simply impossible to buy an inefficient refrigerator. In some states certain kinds of logging practices are outlawed, such as cutting on steep slopes, due to their impact on growth and ecological efficiency. There are regulations on the kinds of fishing equipment that can be used in an effort to reduce by catch; for example, fishing nets that allow sea turtles to escape rather than be drowned. There are also enforced inefficiencies – regulating the kind of gear that can be used – designed to permit regrowth of desired stocks such as requiring the taking of oysters with tongs rather than dragging the bottom for them. The latter practice is especially damaging the marine ecosystems.

As has already been discussed, differential tax and interest rates can be used to shift the composition of demand, and to stimulate the development of technologies and practices that are more efficient. These mechanisms serve to stimulate innovation that goes beyond that accomplished by regulation. As these devices succeed the regulatory floor can be 'moved up,' thus prohibiting, as time goes by, that which is less efficient. The role of public-sector procurement is also important. Public procurement of cars, paper, buildings for purchase or rent, and so on, can reward those who advance service and maintenance efficiency. Forestry practices designed to facilitate regrowth, or to minimize collateral ecological damage, can be certified as we now, albeit imperfectly, have means of determining the sources of rare woods. Regulations, taxes and interest rates, and public-sector procurements thus serve as a nested set of tools in service to the stewardship model.

Similar considerations apply to the human diet. There are two countervailing trends underway at once. On the one hand, as incomes rise, the demand for meat expands so that the total number of animals raised for slaughter is no doubt at unprecedented levels. At the same time the scientific, moral, and religious justifications for human superiority over other species are in substantial retreat. Reducing or eliminating the use of other animals for food would also go a long way toward reducing human pressure on the world's ecosystems, from former tropical forests to grazing on public lands in the western United States. Everything else being equal it would improve human health. It would make more food available to the poor because it would reduce pressure on world grain stocks by allowing grain now fed to animals, or the resources used to produce that grain, to be made available for human use. This is due to the substantial inefficiencies involved in consuming protein in the form of meat. Here is another place where differential taxes on meat as compared with other elements of the human diet can serve to shift the composition of demand in ways that reduce pressures on resources and ecosystems. Precedents abound. Alcoholic beverages are taxed, sometimes heavily, in part to reduce their consumption; while milk is often subsidized to induce children to drink more of it.

EXPANDED STANDING

In many nations standing in a law suit, the ability to be a participant in the suit at all, depends on showing that one is materially effected by the matter at hand. This rule springs, in part at least, to keep cases being so numerous that they clog the courts. It is clear that this rule, as normally interpreted, would prohibit future generations from being parties to suits. But this is too narrow. As human technological capacity and our scientific knowledge have increased we can effect the future more and more, and we can understand that effect much more. In short, we are now aware of the intergenerational effects of much of what we do. Our descendants are highly vulnerable to our present actions. A number of our practices heavily influence and often harm future generations: common examples are the deposition of heavy metals in the environment; wasteful uses of farmland such as paving it; and the alteration of climate; or improper handling of nuclear wastes. The situation is highly asymmetrical: we can do things to them, but they can do nothing to us. Therefore, standing must be extended to them. Of course, actual suits will have to be brought by members of the present generation acting as proxies on behalf of the future, obviously new criteria will have to be developed to determine who has standing to sue in order to keep from overwhelming the courts. The absence of such standards at this time are not sufficient reasons to deny what justice requires.

A related question pertains to standing for other species. In many countries the law already protects nonhumans in a number of ways. We protect rare and endangered species and their habitat; most animals are protected from certain forms of cruelty; and certain farming practices which rely on crowding, confined movement, or force feeding are illegal in some countries. These protections should be expanded and made, if they are not already, the objects of both civil and criminal penalties.

There should also be crimes against the environment itself.[3] These crimes need not be reducible to crimes against persons or their property, though major alterations of ecological systems often entail these damages as well. Failure to discharge our duties to environmental systems should also be the object of criminal sanctions. Of course, alterations of natural systems are inevitable. Every organism alters its environment. But the fiduciary conception defended here requires that these alterations by kept within the range of legitimate human wealth as defined in Chapter 3. A reasonably sized human population is at liberty to protect itself from insect-bourne disease vectors through vaccines that kill viruses, and similar protective measures. We are justified in mounting and sustaining an agriculture capable of providing a safe and reliable food supply. But it is also clear that there are unjustifiable alterations: clear cutting on steep slopes that cause extensive erosion and habitat loss for aquatic and terrestrial creatures alike are clearly prohibited within the fiduciary framework. Release of waste that cannot be assimilated by natural systems should be a criminal offense unless it is unavoidable to protect basic human rights.

COSMOPOLITAN EDUCATION AND RESEARCH

Human equality and stewardship require that toleration be a fundamental virtue. Knowledge of history, other cultures, and the experiences, emotions, and thought processes of other persons are essential to develop a world culture built around equal respect for other people's choices. We must also explicitly educate for stewardship. This will require considerable redirection. In the United States there are numerous institutions, such as the Harvard's Kennedy School of Government, which educate persons who will assume leadership positions in government. They are often taught that the reason government exists can be grounded in the theory of market failures. We considered the defects of this point of view in Chapter 4 and saw how extensively and unfortunately it compressed discourse about the legitimate functions of government. It is not perfectly functioning markets at which we should aim, but stewardship of the commonwealth of life. This would require a curriculum grounded in classic texts on the role and nature of government, including Hobbes *Leviathan*, and Locke's *Second Treatise*, both of which emphasize the role of government in the conservation of human life. But, of course, the anthropocentric features of these texts must be transcended. Substantial education in the biological and physical sciences is necessary to see the complex systems effects of our actions on ourselves and the rest of the living world, toward which we bear fiduciary responsibility.

The idea of the commonwealth of life also has implications for research. Much of our research has concentrated on *homo sapiens* and viewed other living things mainly, or entirely, instrumentally. As a consequence we have failed to learn much about the mental life of other species.[4] But to know how to treat them we have to know more about them. Moving to materials internalization or pollution reduction as the goal of policy will require the development of industrial processes very different from the ones that we now have. There will be much to be done in chemical, electrical, and agricultural engineering. Firms will have to behave differently, and the goals of management will need to be constrained by considerations of the commonwealth of life.

POPULATION AND IMMIGRATION

Within the framework of the commonwealth of life the human population has to be sized to allow for the flourishing of other species in addition to our own. It thus radically broadens the framework proposed by Thomas Malthus,[5] who thought of the issue of human population solely in terms of the ability of humans to supply their needs for food. Malthusian considerations certainly apply in parts of the world at this time. There is simply not enough food to feed the existing human population that already exists in some regions. A number of factors typically lie behind these shortages including civil unrest and wars, lack of income and employment, degradation of soils, mismanagement of water, inefficient agriculture, the disruption of productive agricultural techniques that had been working,[6] and the like. Nevertheless, the aggregate food production in the world, if distributed differently, could, especially if there was a reduction in the amount of meat eaten, adequately feed all persons alive at this time.

But there is no reason to limit the framework to that offered by Malthus. There is no reason to be concerned only with the continuation of human life. From the fiduciary perspective it is evident that current population levels, coupled with incomes and consumption practices, are already much too high. These factors are resulting in a radical loss of the life forms of the earth. Some of the steps already outlined, such as biological surveys and conservation areas, substitution for stewardship, differential loans and taxes, and so on, will serve to mitigate these trends.

But there are just too many people. Even if fully implemented the steps just outlined will be insufficient, for they are largely local in character. They do little to address global problems such as climate destabilization, which is already occurring at a rate too fast for many species to adapt to it. For this reason there will have to be national quotas for substances that are significant factors in the destabilization of global systems. The case of carbon dioxide provides a useful example. Existing global carbon emissions will have to be cut by substantially more than 50 per cent. Obviously, much of this can be achieved with changing technology and consumption patterns, but human-population reduction or stabilization in many countries will need to be part of the response. Population reduction or stabilization will also help to reduce more local pressures such as habitat loss, though substantial reconceptualization of property rights (as set out in Chapter 5) to emphasize the fiduciary dimension of ownership will also have to occur.

Countries that are already outliers in per capita carbon emissions, such as the United States and Canada, and those that are likely to be in gross terms like China and India, have special responsibilities in this regard. For example, those countries experiencing significant immigration pressure should explicitly calculate the role of additional persons in achieving or failing to achieve their emission targets. The carbon emissions of native and immigrant are interchangeable from the viewpoint of world climate. With the fiduciary conception, therefore, domestic population and *net* immigration policies should be made according to a formula such as: carbon emissions per capita multiplied by existing/prospective technologies multiplied by existing/prospective consumption patterns. These constraints will be set by an international treaty designed to reach rough equilibrium between greenhouse gas emissions into the atmosphere and removals from it. The rich countries with little or negative population growth can keep within their targets by reducing consumption per capita, or by changing their technology, and/or reducing their population. The poorer countries that are experiencing rapid population growth can attain their targets by reducing the number of capita below some base line through expanded family planning and through adopting more environmentally benign technologies. The industrial nations have obligations to help in both these respects.

The fiduciary conception does not ratify the high levels of consumption that currently characterize the industrialized countries in making the calculation of appropriate population size. Doing so would allow countries to deny immigration to foreigners because they wanted to maintain wasteful habits of energy, land use, and other forms of consumption. On the contrary, the conception of stewardship economics sets these countries on a course to lower their consumption and reduce the impact of the newly configured consumption within stewardship economics.

In the twentieth century alone the human population has increased by several billion persons. The present situation is not the norm, but a deviation from it. Population reduction is not some distant dream beyond achievement. In most European countries the rate of reproduction is well below replacement. A high priority of those countries with positive rates of growth such as the United States and many of the less developed countries needs to be the use of incentives to eliminate, and in most cases reverse, growth. In many cases reduction of the population through access to birth control, tax and housing incentives, and the like is imperative. There is no right to reproduction if one cannot care directly or indirectly through special programs for the children that one brings into the world. Similarly, societies should limit their overall population to that which can live within the range of legitimate wealth, given the characteristics of their technology. It is clear that countries such as the United States are living way beyond the range of legitimate wealth when viewed from the fiduciary perspective.

With regard to the immigration dimension of population change the fiduciary conception does help us to decide who should be admitted under whatever ceilings a country establishes to protect the global commons and the commonwealth of life within its borders. This will generate a framework for each nation to judge its present and desired consumption patterns and level of population. Policy will have to adjust between the two fiduciary objectives. Since most countries experience some emigration the question is what the net change should be. Here the basic-rights conception comes into play. We are trying to steer a course between the protection of basic rights, and our more general obligations to the common-wealth of life. We seek to limit population in part to protect the commonwealth of life. To discharge the other side of our fiduciary obligations we should give first priority, within whatever overall limit has been established, to those persons whose basic rights are most threatened and which cannot be protected in other ways. This differs from the way immigration is thought of in the growth model, which emphasizes that countries should admit those most likely to contribute to economic growth.[7] Of course, we should continue to discharge our other obligations to protect the basic rights of foreign nationals *in situ* by the means described in the next section of this chapter.

THE ANNUAL REPORT OF THE WORLD'S TRUSTEES

Each year the world's governments should issue a report to the United Nations or similarly situated body reporting on its compliance with fiduciary standards. Its audience should be the other governments and the citizens of the world.

THE WORLD

The desired behavior of nations sketched above is a long way from the one we have. The transition will not be easy because the conduct to be regulated is often that of those who do the regulation. But some steps can be started now, and to some degree are being done already by nongovernmental organizations. To secure the future of our own species and that of the commonwealth of life generally we will need to continue and accelerate trends already underway to establish a new institutional structure, a structure that corresponds to the global state at which problems occur. (A strengthened United Nations Environment Program is a possible avenue for moving in this direction.) In his *This Endangered Planet*, which contains an analysis of the desired world order similar to the one in this book, Richard Falk lists the characteristics of these international institutions as follows:

1. Central political institutions of general authority.
2. Specialized agencies devoted to specific tasks on international coordination.
3. Informal and tacit patterns of coordination among principal world political actors.
4. Transnational and multilateral actors and movements devoted to special tasks or to social and political change.
5. Regional and subregional organizations performing certain tasks of a cooperative nature in relation, especially, to economic and security subject matter.[8]

What the fiduciary perspective does is to provide a framework for thinking about what international institutions we need and how their functions should be specified. Each of the five levels specified above requires the one below it. They can be thought of as types of *transparency*.

First, there is a need to have an overarching set of treaties which set forth the minimal duties of nations to their citizens, the commonwealth of life, and each other.[9] Many of these treaties already exist.[10] Adding to and strengthening international treaties is not a plea for world government. Indeed, there are a number of reasons to think that a world government is undesirable. A government representing over six billion people would ratchet up by several orders of magnitude the feeling that many have in much smaller entities of being lost in the crowd. It would have to function across peoples of diverse histories and cultures. The subject of world government is not under general discussion. Its evolution would require decades, if not centuries, to come about; while the problems of subsistence, security, and stopping the widespread assault on the commonwealth of life are acute and urgent.

The treaties set the terms for actions and their implementation can be entrusted to specialized agencies. This is step two. A number of these already exist concerning matters as diverse as an international postal service, trade, food, scientific exchange, labor, restoration of global commons such as the world's ozone layer, and numerous others. Many of these agencies have been functioning for decades. The fiduciary perspective simply adds to their purview by including stabilization of climate, inventories of biodiversity, farm and forest land, and so on, to the list of matters of concern.

Implementing these diverse treaties leads to level three: the need for co-operation and co-ordination.[11] Falk calls for the creation of a 'Concert of Principal Actors.' This would be a gathering of the major actors in world affairs to supply information for implementing and verifying the treaties and the actions of the specialized agencies under them. It would include governments, corporations, nongovernmental organizations such as the Red Cross and Red Crescent, the International Union for the Conservation of Nature, and the like. There will be a need for the standardization of procedures for data collection and dissemination, the cajoling of those who are remiss in their obligations, the assessments of new and emerging problems. There could be annual meetings of such a Concert, as well as the creation of standing committees.

The fourth needed level is happening spontaneously: the emergence of international groups designed to advance specific agendas. There are groups dedicated to the protection of: human rights against torture and arbitrary confinement; tropical and temperate forests; subsistence rights of indigenous peoples; world wetlands and farmland, and numerous other examples. The fiduciary perspective argued for here provides a framework in which to see these otherwise apparently disparate activities.

Step five, regional co-operation, is also emerging with regard to both economic and security considerations. Trading blocs such as the North American Free Trade Agreement, and the European Union have emerged. Regional security and nonaggression pacts are more and more common. It is now widely recognized that there are international obligations to secure civil order, if necessary by the use of force. As Falk notes:

> The world order appeal of regional organizations is twofold: first, to move foreign policy and international relations beyond the nation state, and second, to create a stepping stone to an overall or central organization of world affairs. In the first context, the regional buildup dilutes the affiliation of the individual to the national government, and thereby weakens traditional forms of patriotism, softens interstate rivalry, and may diminish the prospects of warfare. In the second context, the experience with supranationalism supports the further transition to a more unitary system of world order.[12]

Many of these regional institutions have increasing environmental responsibilities such as compacts between the United States and Canada concerning management of the Great Lakes.

With these generic institutions of transparency in mind here are some suggestions about how nations can move toward a world in which trustee states discharge their fiduciary obligations.

SECURING PEACE

The primary reason that Locke urges the establishment of government to begin with is to put a stop to the 'inconveniences of nature.' The widespread civil disorders of our time, often the result of revenge cycles stretching back decades or even centuries, are taking the lives of millions, disrupting agriculture and other forms of commerce, undercutting education, destroying or altering the habitat of numerous other species, and in some cases directly killing rare and endangered plants and animals. It is a primary duty of the international community to intervene in these conflicts, stopping them by force if necessary.[13] International peace-securing and keeping efforts already underway are important steps in discharging this duty. In many cases the countries in which the conflict is occurring may need to become reconfigured on the basis of plebiscites taken to reflect the consent of the governed. The international community should publicize the country, city, and manufacturer of arms used in these conflicts. The argument of this book also puts limits on the use of force. For force to be justified there must be clear systematic violations of the duties of states to protect the rights of their citizens and the commonwealth of life.

FOREIGN ECONOMIC ASSISTANCE

The fundamental default obligation that we have toward the citizens of other nations is to see that their three basic rights are secure. One aspect of this security is economic particularly with regard to subsistence rights. In many cases securing this may require no action at all. Indeed, it may require forbearing from actions that would impair subsistence rights. For example, shifting to an export crop such as flowers may result in the lowering of nutritional status of those displaced from the land.

Assistance beyond that oriented to basic rights may be laudatory, depending on its effects, but it is not morally mandatory. This contrasts sharply with other conceptions: the growth model, utilitarianism, and the capability school. It obviously goes beyond communitarian theories which can limit obligations to members of one's group.[14] We don't need to linger for long over the first two options.

The goal of foreign assistance in the growth model is to foster economic growth, and for them foreign assistance should be judged by its success or failure in reaching that goal. We saw in Chapter 3 that this model should give way to a stewardship economics. We need an economics that can answer our elementary questions. The current growth framework cannot help us to decide what we owe to others. This is not to say, of course, that certain kinds of economic growth might not be instrumental in securing one or more of the basic rights. But the rights conception sets the goal and serves as a means of judging, along with respect for the commonwealth of life, if our obligations to others have been discharged.

Nor is utilitarianism, which we also considered in Chapter 3 in the context of the goal of efficiency, a serious contender. With respect to foreign assistance Peter Singer formulates this principle in his seminal essay 'Famine, Affluence, and Morality,' as follows: 'if it is in our power to prevent something very bad from happening, without thereby sacrificing anything else morally significant, we ought, morally, to do it.'[15] Singer's argument was developed in response to the famines of the early 1970s. He argued that the rich have obligations to give assistance to those threatened by food shortages. Of course, the human-rights element of the fiduciary conception leads to the same conclusion since famine is a clear violation of subsistence rights. But Singer's account of obligation is much too open ended in two ways. First, 'something very bad from happening' is unnecessarily vague in a way that the rights conception is not. In this way it has an inadequate conception of the good. Second, it entails an inadequate account of obligation. It creates a set of duties to respond to negative results of any kind, brought about by anyone, anywhere. It transfers moral autonomy from the agent to the world at large.[16] If someone in a distant land is going to do something bad to someone else we would, on Singer's formulation, be obligated to try to prevent it if we could. There are no limits on obligation other than 'I cannot'. It thus conflicts with the right to moral and political choice: the right to order our own lives in accordance with our own values.

We saw in Chapter 1 that Nobel Laureate Sen's capabilities approach while a distinct improvement over neo-classical conceptions of the goals of foreign assistance also has serious shortcomings. These were (1) a long list of what is desired, without any priorities – an inadequate account of the good; (2) lack of institutional context which offers an account of who has the corresponding duties; and (3) and this problem is in common with Singer's account – it creates too many duties. If I seriously believed that I had an obligation to maximize the capabilities of people around the globe it would leave little or no time for my own projects and purposes. In a word, as an account of development *assistance* it requires too much. This does not, of course, mean that people should not flourish as they and their society define flourishing; it just means that there is no international obligation to help bring this about beyond what is required by the basic-rights conception.[17]

TRADE

Seen from the fiduciary perspective world trade should be characterized as constrained exchange. Indeed, rather than allowing trade to undercut sovereignty, as it does in the neo-classical free-trade regime, it can be a means of restoring robustness. A number of limits should be applied to it:

1. There should be minimum standards to protect the three basic rights. Labor laws that protect children from exploitation and allow for education are essential if we take the requirements of freedom of choice seriously. Minimum working conditions which specify levels of noise, air, and other forms of pollution should be set out to protect the bodily integrity of workers. Minimum levels of nutrition should be specified relative to age, work and other forms of effort, and other factors.

2. Minimum standards of air and water pollution outside the workplace should be set.

3. The movement of capital should be restricted, but by no means prohibited, to preserve the ability of states to control their own domestic economic policy so that basic rights can be protected in times of economic turmoil. In a way that parallels the neo-classical conception trade sanctions should be used to assure that countries meet the fiduciary standards of transparent sovereignty.

4. States should be able to restrict goods (through both tariffs and quotas) from other countries that are produced at prices lower than they could be produced in the receiving country due to a subsidy incompatible with fiduciary standards. For example, in industrial plants that have inadequate air-pollution controls workers subsidize production with their lungs. Countries that allow logging on steep slopes often subsidize their production with their fisheries and with abundant losses to the commonwealth of life.

5. Certain goods should not be sold at all, adding to the list of things already withheld from the market. This list should, and to some degree already does, include persons, plants and animals from threatened species, unless the sale is connected with a program designed to preserve the species itself. For example, a limited, highly regulated trade in ivory may be justified to preserve the elephants through creating financial incentives for their conservation. The pending ban on the sale of land mines should be ratified by all countries.

6. Once it is properly inventoried, farmland should be withheld from any market which intended to convert it. Forestry and fishery practices should be restricted in the kind and location of harvesting techniques to assure growth and eco-logical efficiency.

7. Sources of global dis-equilibria such as carbon emissions from the process of trade itself should be allocated against some nations' quota – perhaps that in which the vessels are flagged.

From the neo-classical perspective the suggestions listed above will be criticized as inefficient and as recipes for the perpetuation of poverty. They are inefficient because each of the suggestions listed above will, to the degree that they are effective, rule out certain exchanges that people would otherwise make. Net satisfaction will be less than in a world that did not have these restrictions. But this is true of any set of rules that limit voluntary exchanges. As we saw in Chapter 4 society neither does nor should aim at perfectly functioning, utility-optimizing markets.

The charge of inducing poverty is more serious. It may be argued that some countries may choose to set their standards below international thresholds in order to attract employment opportunities for persons who would otherwise be destitute. It is better to have a job at a low wage in a polluted plant than to have no job at all and be spending one's days malnourished on the street. But this objection to minimum standards assumes the neo-classical conception of transparent sovereignty that there are no other transboundary obligations. The fiduciary conception makes the satisfaction of the three basic rights an international responsibility. And there are a number of means to satisfy these rights. Under the provisions of the Montreal Protocol less developed nations are supplied with funds and technical assistance in meeting the mandate of curtailing and then eliminating substances that deplete the earth's ozone layer. Similar arrangements could be put in place to meet the minimal standards set out above, financed in part by taxes discussed in the next section. On the fiduciary conception no nation is an island, no person abandoned completely to the vagaries of market forces.

One thing is obvious: economics is too important to be left to economics alone. Given the nature of economic education in much of the West, and the tendency to undersupply the very institutions that are needed for the market itself to work, we will have to restructure graduate education to compensate for these shortcomings.

INTERNATIONAL TAXES

There are a number of international taxes justified within the fiduciary perspective. First, we need international taxes for at least some minimal income security; and to finance the research, promulgation, and enforcement of environmental standards. Second, we have already seen that international markets have been under supplied with the institutions that make them work. International enforcement of antitrust, currency stabilization, and the like – just what is needed to keep the neo-classical framework itself going – requires taxes to support these institutions. Third, use of the global commons such as the atmosphere and oceans should be taxed. Revenues could be distributed to poorer persons for investment in noncarbon-intensive technologies, or given as means of securing subsistence rights, or more generally to discharge their twofold fiduciary duties. Fourth, to preserve the strength of nations there should be an international tax on capital movements. It would be particularly appropriate to use these taxes to support those who have lost their means of subsistence due to globalization. Fifth, to the degree that the export of undesirable products such as weapons and cigarettes are not prohibited they could be heavily taxed to increase the incentives against their use. Revenues could be distributed to those harmed by the exchange of the taxed good. For example, revenues from taxes on cigarettes could be used to care for those who get smoking-related diseases. Revenues from taxes on weapons could be used to care for those injured in wars, to finance resettlement of refugees and the like.

A DECLARATION OF STEWARDSHIP
Parallel to, or perhaps subsuming the United Nations Declaration on Human Rights, there should be a declaration of stewardship. It should enumerate the responsibilities of the world's nations as stewards, and set up ways that each nation can demonstrate that it has observed these norms.

LISTING NONREPORTING NATIONS
Nations that do not file their trustee reports should be listed in a widely available public report. Such a report could be distributed by the United Nations, the International Red Cross or similar institution.

RELYING ON THE INDEPENDENTS
There are already groups such as Amnesty International, the Nature Conservancy, Friends of the Earth, the Red Cross, and Red Crescent, and many others who provide independent information with respect to the performance of the world's governments as trustees. The reports of these institutions should be compiled into an annual report *on* the world's trustees pointing up any conflicts between the self-reports of nations and the findings of others. Nations which do not file such reports should be the objects of especially intense study.

THE WORLD COURT
The World Court should be strengthened and a category of crimes added under the heading of crimes against nature. The filling and draining of wetlands, the extinction of species, siltation of streams and the like should be prosecutable in court. Future generations and nonhumans should be given standing in these proceedings.

FROM TWIGS TO STICKS
Additional sanctions ranging from refusal to allow participation in Olympic games and other highly visible public events, trade sanctions and embargoes, to the use of multi-national peace-keeping, and in rare cases invasion forces should be used to bring about compliance with the

158

standard of transparent trusteeship. Obviously one should begin at the least violent end of the range of sanctions. Many of the industrialized nations, and increasingly the nonindustrialised nations, including, but not limited to, the United States, are threatening the stability of the world's climate system. The international community, including the independents, should apply sanctions against the violating nations.

NOTES

1. Jonathan Weiner, *The Beak of the Finch*.
2. Alston Chase, *Playing God in Yellowstone: the destruction of America's first national park*.
3. See, for example, the Law Reform Commission of Canada, *Working Paper 44: Crimes Against the Environment*.
4. Donald R. Griffin, *Animal Minds*.
5. Thomas Malthus, *On Population*.
6. George Monbiot, 'The Tragedy of Enclosure,' *Scientific American*, January 1994, p. 159.
7. US Immigration and Nationality Act, Title II – Immigration, Chapter 1 – Selection System, Act 203 – Allocation of Immigration Visas, (b).
8. Richard A. Falk, *This Endangered Planet*, pp. 314–15.
9. See Lawrence E. Susskind, *Environmental Diplomacy: Negotiating More Effective Global Agreements* for a discussion of ways to strengthen the system of global environmental treaties.
10. Ibid., p. 15. Susskind lists examples of global environmental treaties: International Convention for the Regulation of Whaling; Antarctic Treaty; Treaty Banning Nuclear Weapons Tests in the Atmosphere, in Outer Space and Underwater; Convention on Wetlands of International Importance Especially as Waterfowl Habitat; Convention on the Prevention of Marine Pollution by Dumping of Wastes and Other Matter; Convention Concerning the Protection of the World Cultural and National Heritage; Convention on International Trade in Endangered Species; International Convention for the Prevention of Pollution from Ships; Convention on the Conservation of Migratory Species of Wild Animals; Convention on Long-Range Transboundary Air Pollution; United Nations Convention on the Law of the Sea; Vienna Convention for the Protection of the Ozone Layer; Convention on the Control of Transboundary Movements of Hazardous Wastes and their Disposal; Biodiversity Convention; and the Convention on Climate Change.
11. Falk, *This Endangered Planet*, pp. 327–9.
12. Falk, ibid., p. 336.
13. See Anthony Clark Arend and Robert J. Beck, *International Law and the Use of Force* for a discussion of whether standards governing the international use of force have moved from a standard of securing peace such as set forth in the United Nations Charter to a new standard of using force to remove illegitimate regimes.

14. Daly and Cobb, *For the Common Good.*
15. Peter Singer, 'Famine, Affluence, and Morality,' in William Aiken and Hugh LaFollette (eds), *World Hunger and Morality*, 2nd edn, p. 31.
16. Bernard Williams, 'Critique of Utilitarianism,' in Smart and Williams, *Utilitarianism For and Against.*
17. The tripartite rights conception also differs from global Rawlsianism as expressed in Beitz' *Political Theory and International Relations.* Beitz' interpretation of the global implications of Rawls' *A Theory of Justice* is that there is a transnational duty to maximize the position of the least advantaged representative person with regard to an index of primary goods including income. There are many reasons not to accept Rawls' analysis even within the nation state. One of them is to make the argument for the difference principle work Rawls has to embrace a determinism that denies people any role in influencing their share of contested goods. See, for example, p. 15 of *A Theory of Justice.* There is thus a symmetry between the views of the extreme right, who deny that the rich have any obligation to help the poor (e.g. Nozick) and Rawls' view which offers no account of how the poor are obligated to help themselves. Thomas Pogge's *Realizing Rawls* says only that international Rawlsianism requires that we need to 'preclude institutions that tend to produce severe deprivations' (p. 272). Pogge argues that insisting on a global maximin (maximising the position of the least advantaged person) principle would interfere with the rights of states under Rawls' first principle to arrange their own economic institutions. In practice, his position is somewhat similar to that defended in this book. In my view, the basic-rights strategy of Locke and Shue is a much more straightforward route to this conclusion.

BIBLIOGRAPHY

Ackerman, Frank, Kiron, David, Goodwin, Neva R., Harris, Jonathan M., and Gallagher, Kevin (eds) (1997), *Human Well-Being and Economic Goals*, Washington, DC: Island Press.

Aiken, William and LaFollette, Hugh, (1996), *World Hunger and Morality*, 2nd edn, Upper Saddle River, NJ: Prentice-Hall.

Anderson, Terry Lee and Leal, Donald R. (1991), *Free Market Environmentalism*, San Francisco: Pacific Research Institute for Public Policy.

Aquinas, Thomas, Saint (1950), *Summa Theologica*, Stanford, CA: Stanford University Press.

Archer, John (ed.) (1994), *Male Violence*, London: Routledge.

Arend, Anthony Clark and Beck, Robert J. (1993), *International Law and the Use of Force*, London: Routledge.

Aristotle (1992), *Politics*, Viking Press.

Aristotle (1998), *Ethics*, Dover Publications.

Ashcraft, Richard (1986), *Revolutionary Politics and Locke's Two Treatises of Government*, Princeton, NJ: Princeton University Press.

Ashcraft, Richard (1987), *Locke's Two Treatises of Government*, London: Allen and Unwin.

Barry, Brian (1965), *Political Argument*, London: Routledge and Kegan Paul.

Barry, Brian (1983), 'Intergenerational Justice in Energy Policy,' in Douglas MacLean and Peter G, Brown (eds.), *Energy and the Future*, Totowa, NJ: Rowman and Littlefield.

Beitz, Charles (1979), *Political Theory and International Relations*, Princeton, NJ: Princeton University Press.

Bell, Daniel (1976), *The Cultural Contradictions of Capitalism*, New York: Basic Books.

Bentham, Jeremy (1962), *Anarchial Fallacies: Being an Examination of the Declaration of Rights Issued during the French Revolution,* vol. 2 of *Works of Jeremy Bentham*, John Bowring (ed.), New York: Russell and Russell.

Berger, John J. (1985), *Restoring the Earth: How Americans Are Working to Renew Our Damaged Environment*, New York: Knopf/Random House.

Berlin, Isaiah (1967), 'Two Concepts of Liberty,' in Anthony Quinton (ed.), *Political Philosophy*, Oxford: Oxford University Press.

Berry, Wendell (1977), *The Unsettling of America: Culture and Agriculture*, New York: Random House.

Braudel, Fernand (1992), *The Structures of Everyday Life: The Limits of the Possible (Civilization and Capitalism: 15th–18th Century)*, Berkeley: University of California Press.

Bridgman, Raymond L, (1972), *The First Book of Law*, New York: Garland Publishing, Inc.

Bronner, Stephen E. (1995), 'Internationalism in Our Time,' *Global Justice*, vol. 1, no. 1, Spring, pp. 5–9.

Brown, Peter G. (1979), '… in the National Interest,' in Peter G. Brown and Douglas MacLean (eds.), *Human Rights and US Foreign Policy: Principles and Applications*, Lexington: Lexington Books.

Brown, Peter G. (1994), *Restoring the Public Trust*, Boston: Beacon Press.

Burtt, Edwin A. (ed.) (1939), *The English Philosophers from Bacon to Mill*, New York: The Modern Library.

Bury, John B. (1932), *The Idea of Progress: An inquiry into its Origin and Growth*, New York: Dover Publications.

Carson, Rachel (1962), *Silent Spring*, Boston, MA: Houghton Mifflin.

Cavanagh, John, Wysham, Daphne, and Arruda, Marcos (eds) (1994), *Beyond Bretton Woods: Alternatives to the Global Economic Order*, London: Pluto Press.

Chase, Alton (1986), *Playing God in Yellowstone: The Destruction of America's First National Park*, Boston, MA: Atlantic Monthly Press.

Chase, Alton (1995), *In a Dark Wood: The Fight over Forests and the Rising Tyranny of Ecology*, Boston, MA: Houghton Mifflin Co.

Coase, Ronald (1960), 'The Problem of Social Cost,' *The Journal of Law and Economics*, vol. 3, October, pp. 1–44.

Cobb, Clifford, Halstead, Ted, and Rowe, Jonathan (1995), 'If the GDP is Up, Why is America Down?', *The Atlantic Monthly*, October, pp. 59–78.

Cobb, John, 'Ecology, Ethics, and Theology,' in Herman E. Daly and Kenneth Townsend (eds) (1993), *Valuing the Earth: Economics, Ecology, Ethics*, Cambridge, MA: The MIT Press.

Commission on Environmental Law of IUCN – The World Conservation Union (1995), *International Covenant on Environment and Development: Environmental Policy and Law Paper no. 31*, Gland, Switzerland: IUCN.

Cooper, Richard N. (1994), *Environment and Resource Policies for the*

World Economy, Washington, DC: The Brookings Institution.

Crocker, David A. (1992), 'Functioning and Capability: The Foundations of Sen's and Nussbaum's Development Ethic,' *Political Theory*, vol. 20, no. 4, November, pp. 584–612.

Crocker, David A. (1996), 'Hunger, Capability, and Development,' in William Aiken and Hugh LaFollette (eds), *World Hunger and Morality*, 2nd edn, Englewood Cliffs, NJ: Prentice-Hall.

Cronon, William (1983), *Changes in the Land: Indians, Colonists, and the Ecology of New England*, New York: Hill and Wang.

Daly, Herman E. (1991), *Steady-state Economics: The Economics of Biophysical Equilibrium and Moral Growth*, 2nd edn, Washington, DC: Island Press.

Daly, Herman E. (1996), *Beyond Growth: The Economics of Sustainable Development*, Boston, MA: Beacon Press.

Daly, Herman E. and Cobb, John B. Jr (1989), *For the Common Good*, Boston, MA: Beacon Press.

Danah, Zohar (1990), *The Quantum Self*, New York: Morrow.

Daniels, Norman (1979), 'Wide Reflective Equilibrium and Theory Acceptance in Ethics,' 76, *The Journal of Philosophy*, no. 5, pp. 256–82.

Darwin, Charles [1859, 1871], *The Origin of the Species and the Descent of Man*, New York: The Modern Library.

Denise, Susan Hankin (1985), 'Regulating the Sale of Human Organs,' *Virginia Law Review*, vol. 71, no. 6, September, pp. 1015–38.

Dower, Nigel (1998), *World Ethics: The New Agenda*, Edinburgh: Edinburgh University Press.

Duchin, Faye and Lange, Glenn-Marie (1994), *The Future of the Environment: Ecological Economics and Technological Change*, New York: Oxford University Press.

Dunn, John (1985), 'The Concept of "Trust" in the Politics of John Locke,' in Richard Rorty, J. B. Schneewind and Quentin Skinner (eds), *Philosophy in History*, Cambridge: Cambridge University Press.

Einstein, Albert (1961), *Relativity: The Special and the General Theory*, New York: Crown Publishers, Inc.

Engel, J. Ronald and Engel, Joan Gibb (eds) (1990), *Ethics of Environment and Development: Global Challenge, International Response*, London: Belhaven Press.

Engels, Friedrich (1968) [1845], *The Conditions of the Working Class in England*, Stanford: Stanford University Press.

Epstein, Richard (1985), *Takings*, Cambridge, MA: Harvard University Press.

Epstein, Richard (1987), 'Takings: Descent and Resurrection,' *The Supreme Court Review*, vol. 1, pp. 1–45.

Esty, Daniel C. (1994), *Greening the GATT: Trade, Environment, and the Future*, Washington, DC: Institute for International Economics.

Falk, Richard A. (1971), *This Endangered Planet: Prospects and Proposals for Human Survival*, New York: Random House.

Faulkner, Robert K. (1993), *Francis Bacon and the Project of Progress*, Lanham, MD: Rowan and Littlefield Publishers, Inc.

Flader, Susan L. and Callicott, J. Baird (eds) (1991), *The River of the Mother of God and Other Essays by Aldo Leopold*, Madison, WI: The University of Wisconsin Press.

Forman, Michael (1995), 'National Minorities and National Self-Determination: Confronting an Old Debate,' *Global Justice*, vol. 1, no. 1, Spring, pp. 25–38.

Foundation for the Progress of Humanity in France (1993), *Platform for a Responsible and United World*, Paris: Foundation for the Progress of Humanity.

Friedman, Milton (1962), *Capitalism and Freedom*, Chicago: University of Chicago Press.

Gedicks, Al (1993), *The New Resource Wars: Native and Environmental Struggles Against Multinational Corporations*, Boston, MA: South End Press.

Geisel, Theodore Seuss (1971), *The Lorax*, New York: Random House.

Goodin, Robert E. (1985), *Protecting the Vulnerable: A Reanalysis of Our Social Responsibilities*, Chicago: University of Chicago Press.

Gough, J. W. (1973), *John Locke's Political Philosophy*, Oxford: Clarendon Press.

Graff, J. de V. (1967), *Theoretical Welfare Economics*, Cambridge: Cambridge University Press.

Griffin, Donald R (1992), *Animal Minds*, Chicago: University of Chicago Press.

Guha, Ramachandra (1989), 'Radical American Environmentalism and Wilderness Preservation: A Third World Critique,' *Environmental Ethics*, Spring.

Hardin, Garrett (1968), 'The Tragedy of the Commons,' *Science*, 162, pp. 1243–8.

Harris, Glenn R., King, Leslie A., and Clary, Mary Beth (1998), 'Growth Management for Environmental Protection in the USA,' *Journal of Environmental Management*, vol. 27, pp. 53–68.

Hart, H. L. A. (1979) 'Between Utility and Rights,' *Columbia Law Review*, 828.

Hays, Samuel P. (1959), *Conservation and the Gospel of Efficiency: The Progressive Conservation Movement, 1890–1920*, Cambridge, MA: Harvard University Press.

Heilbroner, Robert L. (1970), *The Making of Economic Society*, Englewood Cliffs, NJ: Prentice-Hall.

Hoffman, Stanley (1981), *Duties Beyond Borders: On the Limits and Possibilities of Ethical International Politics*, Syracuse, NY: Syracuse University Press.

Hollings, C. S. (1992), 'A Cross-Scale Morphology, Geometry, and Dynamics of Ecosystems,' *Ecological Monographs*, vol. 62, no. 4, pp. 447–502.

Hollings, C. S. (1994), 'An Ecologist View of the Malthusian Conflict,' in Kerstin Lindahl-Kiessling and Hans Landberg (eds.), *Population, Economic Development, and the Environment*, New York: Oxford University Press.

Kant, Immanuel (1963), 'Duties to Animals and Spirits,' in *Lectures on Ethics*, trans. Louis Enfield, New York: Harper and Row.

Katz, Michael L. and Rosen, Harvey S. (1998), *Microeconomics*, Boston, MA: Irwin/McGraw-Hill.

Kellogg, William W. and Schware, Robert (1982), 'Society, Science and Climate Change,' *Foreign Affairs*, Summer, pp. 1076–109.

Kenan, Peter B. (ed.) (1994), *Managing the World Economy: Fifty Years After Bretton Woods*, Washington, DC: Institute for International Economics.

Kennan, F. George (1985–6), 'Morality and Foreign Policy,' *Foreign Affairs*, Winter, pp. 205–18.

Keohane, Robert O. and Nye, Joseph S. (1977), *Power and Independence: World Politics in Transition*, Boston: Little, Brown and Company.

Keynes, John Maynard (1964), *The General Theory of Employment, Interest, and Money*, San Diego: Harcourt Brace and Company.

Keynes, John Maynard (1988), *The Economic Consequences of the Peace*, New York: Penguin Books.

Kneese, Allen, V. (1971), 'Analysis of Environmental Pollution,' in Peter Bohm and Allen V. Kneese (eds), *The Economics of Environment*, London: Macmillan.

Kopp, Raymond, Krupnick, Alan, and Toman, Michael (1997), 'Cost-Benefit Analysis and Regulatory Reform,' *Human and Ecological Risk Assessment*, vol. 3, no. 5, pp. 787–852.

Korten, David C. (1990), *Getting to the 21st Century: Voluntary Action and the Global Agenda*, West Hartford, CT: Kumarian Press.

Krueger, Anne O. (1990), 'Free Trade is the Best Policy,' in Robert Z. Lawrence and Charles Schultze (eds), *An American Trade Strategy: Options for the 1990s*, Washington, DC: Brookings Institution.

Krugman, Paul R, and Obstfeld, Maurice (1994), *International Economics: Theory and Policy*, 3rd edn, New York: Harper Collins College Publishers.

Lang, Tim and Hines, Colin (1993), *The New Protectionism: Protecting the Future Against Free Trade*, New York: The New Press.

Large, Donald W. (1986), 'The Land Law of Scotland – A Comparison with American and English Concepts,' *Environmental Law*, vol. 17, no. 1, pp. 1–41.

Lasch, Christopher (1991), *The True and Only Heaven: Progress and its Critics*, New York: Norton.

Laslett, Peter (1965), *The World We Have Lost*, New York: Scribner.

Law Reform Commission of Canada (1985), *Working Paper 44: Crimes Against the Environment*, Ottawa: Law Reform Commission of Canada.

Leakey, Richard (1982), *The Making of Mankind*, London: Sphere Books.

Lekachman, Robert (1966), *The Age of Keynes*, New York: Random House.

Leopold, Aldo (1949), *A Sand County Almanac*, New York: Oxford University Press.

Lichtenberg, Judith (1981), 'National Boundaries and Moral Boundaries,' in Peter G. Brown and Henry Shue (eds), *Boundaries: National Autonomy and its Limits*, Totowa, NJ: Rowman and Littlefield.

Locke, John (1988), *Two Treatises of Government*, Cambridge: Cambridge University Press.

Lorenz, Konrad (1966), *On Aggression*, New York: Harcourt, Brace and World.

McFarlane, Robert C. (1994), *Special Trust*, New York: Cadell and Davies.

MacIntyre, Alasdair (1981), *After Virtue*, Notre Dame: University of Notre Dame Press.

Macpherson, C. B. (1962), *The Political Theory of Possessive Individualism*, Oxford: Clarendon Press.

Malthus, Thomas (1976), *On Population*, W. W. Norton and Co.

Marco, Gino J., Hollingworth, Robert M. and Durham, William (1987), *Silent Spring Revisited*, Washington, DC: American Chemical Society.

Marx, Karl (1980), *The Economic and Philosophic Manuscripts of 1844*, International Publishers.

Merchant, Carolyn (1980), *The Death of Nature: Women, Ecology, and the Scientific Revolution*, San Francisco: Harper and Row.

Midgley, Mary (1983), 'Duties Concerning Islands,' in Robert Elliot and Arran Gare (eds), *Environmental Philosophy: A Collection of Readings*, University Park, PA: Pennsylvania State University Press.

Mill, John Stuart (1939), *Utilitarianism*, in *The English Philosophers from Bacon to Mill*, New York: Modern Library.

Mill, John Stuart (1987), *Utilitarianism,* in John Stuart Mill and Jeremy Bentham, *Utilitarianism and Other Essays*, Middlesex, England: Penguin Press.

Monbiot, George (1994), 'The Tragedy of Enclosure,' *Scientific American*, January, p. 159.

Mowat, Farley (1984), *Sea of Slaughter*, Boston: Atlantic Monthly Press.

Mueller, Dennis (1979), *Public Choice*, Cambridge: Cambridge University Press.

Mumford, Lewis (1938), *Culture of Cities*, New York: Harcourt, Brace and Company.

Naess, Arne (1989), *Ecology, community and lifestyle: Outline of an Ecosophy*, Cambridge: Cambridge University Press.

Nash, James A. (1991), *Loving Nature: Ecological Integrity and Christian Responsibility*, Nashville: Abingdon Press.

Nash, Roderick (1989), *The Rights of Nature: A History of Environmental Ethics*, Madison: University of Wisconsin Press.

Nearing, Helen and Nearing, Scott (1970), *Living the Good Life: How to Live Sanely and Simply in a Troubled World*, New York: Schocken Books.

Nelson, Robert H. (1991), *Reaching for Heaven on Earth: The Theological Meaning of Economics*, Savage, MD: Rowman and Littlefield Publications.

Newton, Sir Isaac (1972) [1726], *Philosophiae naturalis principia mathematica*, 3rd edn, Cambridge, MA: Harvard University Press.

Nisbet, Robert A. (1980), *History of the Idea of Progress*, New York: Basic Books.

Nordhaus, William D. (1994), *Managing the Global Commons: The Economics of Climate Change*, Cambridge, MA: MIT Press.

Norgaard, Richard B. (1994), *Development Betrayed: The End of Progress and a Coevolutionary Revisioning of the Future*, London: Routledge.

North, Douglass Cecil (1981), *Structure and Change in Economic History*, New York: Norton.

Norton, Bryan (1987), *Why Preserve Natural Variety?* Princeton: Princeton University Press.

Norton, Bryan (1991), *Toward Unity Among Environmentalists*, Oxford: Oxford University Press.

Nozick, Robert (1974), *Anarchy, State and Utopia*, New York: Basic Books.

Nussbaum, Martha (1998), 'The Good as Discipline, as Freedom,' in David A. Crocker and Toby Linden (eds), *Ethics of Consumption: The Good Life, Justice, and Global Stewardship*, Lanham, MD: Rowman and Littlefield Publishers, Inc.

Nussbaum, Martha and Sen, Amartya (eds) (1993), *The Quality of Life*, Oxford: Clarendon Press.

Odum, E. P. (1969), 'The Strategy of Ecosystem Development,' *Science*, vol. 164, 18 April, pp. 26–70.

Ostrom, Elinor (1990), *Governing the Commons: The Evolution of Institutions for Collective Action*, Cambridge: Cambridge University Press.

Parfit, Derek (1983), 'Energy Policy and the Further Future: The Social Discount Rate,' in Douglas MacLean and Peter G. Brown (eds), *Energy and the Future*, Totowa, NJ: Rowman and Littlefield.

Pearce, David (ed.) (1997), *The MIT Dictionary of Modern Economics*, Cambridge, MA: The MIT Press.

Penrose, Edith (1995), *The Theory of the Growth of the Firm*, Oxford: Oxford University Press.

Pinchot, Gifford (1914), *The Training of a Forester*, New York: Lippincott Publishing Co. Inc.

Pogge, Thomas (1989), *Realizing Rawls*, Ithaca, NY: Cornell University Press.

Polanyi, Karl (1944), *The Great Transformation*, Boston, MA: Beacon Press.

Prigogine, Ilya (1997), *The End of Certainty: Time, Chaos, and the New Laws of Nature*, New York: Free Press.

Rabkin, Jeremy (1998), *Why Sovereignty Matters*, Washington, DC: The AEI Press.

Rachels, James (1990), *Created from Animals: The Moral Implications of Darwinism*, New York: Oxford University Press.

Ramakrishna, Kilaparti and Woodwell, George M. (eds) (1993), *World Forests for the Future: Their Use and Conservation*, New Haven: Yale University Press.

Rawls, John (1971), *A Theory of Justice*, Cambridge, MA: Belknap Press.

Regan, Tom and Singer, Peter (1989), *Animal Rights and Human Obligations*, 2nd edn, Englewood Cliffs, NJ: Prentice Hall.

Reice, Seth R. (1994), 'Nonequilibrium Determinants of Biological Community Structure,' *American Scientist*, vol. 82, September–October, pp. 424–35.

Reisner, Marc (1986), *Cadillac Desert: The American West and Its Disappearing Water*, New York: Penguin Books.

Repetto, Robert (1992), 'Accounting for Environmental Assets,' *Scientific American*, June.

Ricardo, David (1951), *Principles of Political Economy and Taxation*, Sraffa Edition, Cambridge: Cambridge University Press.

Richards, David A. J. (1983), 'Contractarian Theory, Intergenerational Justice, and Energy Policy,' in Douglas MacLean and Peter G. Brown (eds), *Energy and the Future*, Totowa, NJ: Rowman and Littlefield.

Robert, Karl-Henrik, Holmberg, John, and Eriksson, Karl-Erik (1994), 'Socio-ecological Principles for a Sustainable Society,' a paper presented at the International Symposium 'Down to Earth: Practical

Applications of Ecological Economics,' 24–28 October, in Heredia, Costa Rica.

Rockefeller, Steven C. and Elder, John C. (1990), *Spirit and Nature: Visions of Interdependence*, Middlebury, VT: Christian A, Johnson Memorial Gallery.

Rodrik, Dani (1997), *Has Globalization Gone Too Far?* Washington, DC: Institute for International Economics.

Ruff, Larry E. (1977), 'The Economic Common Sense of Pollution,' in Robert Dorfman and Nancy F, Dorfman (eds), *Economics of the Environment: Selected Readings*, W. W. Norton and Co.

Ruth, John L. (1985), *A Quiet and Peaceable Life: An Account of the Plain People*, Intercourse, PA: Good Books.

Sagoff, Mark (1983), 'At the Shrine of Our Lady of Fatima or Why Political Questions Are Not All Economic,' in Donald Sherer and Thomas Attig (eds), *Ethics and the Environment*, Englewood Cliffs, NJ: Prentice Hall.

Sagoff, Mark (1988), *The Economy of the Earth: Philosophy, Law and the Environment*, Cambridge: Cambridge University Press.

Sahlins, Marshall D. (1972), *Stone Age Economics*, Chicago: Aldine-Atherton.

Sandel, Michael (1982), *Liberalism and the Limits of Justice*, New York: Cambridge University Press.

Santayana, George (1962), *Reason in Religion: Volume III of the Life of Reason, or The Phases of Human Progress*, New York: Collier Books.

Sax, Joseph L. (1988), 'Property Rights in the US Supreme Court: A Status Report,' *Journal of Environmental Law*, vol. 7, no. 139, pp. 139–54.

Sax, Joseph L. (1998), 'Legal and Policy Challenges of Environmental Restoration,' a paper presented at 'Wolves and Human Communities: Biology, Politics, and Ethics,' American Museum of Natural History, New York, 21–23 October.

Schaller, Neill (1993), 'The Concept of Agricultural Sustainability,' *Agriculture, Ecosystems and Environment*, vol. 46.

Schelling, Thomas C. (1995), 'Intergenerational Discounting,' *Energy Policy*, vol. 23, no. 4/5, pp. 395–401.

Schlessinger, Arthur Jr (1976), 'National Interests and Moral Absolutes,' in E. LeFever (ed.), *Ethics and World Politics: Four Perspectives*, Baltimore, MD: Johns Hopkins University Press.

Schuck, Peter H. (1984), 'The Transformation of Immigration Law,' *Columbia Law Review*, vol. 84, no. 1, January, pp. 1–90.

Schweitzer, Albert (1933), *Out of My Life and Thought*, New York: Henry Holt and Company.

Schweitzer, Albert (1969), *Reverence for Life*, New York: Harper and Row.

Schweitzer, Albert (1987), *The Philosophy of Civilization*, Buffalo, NY: Prometheus Books.

Sen, Amartya (1990), 'Development as Capability Expansion,' in Keith Griffin and John Knight (eds), *Human Development and the International Development Strategy for the 1990s*, Basingstoke, Hampshire: Macmillan.

Sen, Amartya (1995), 'Gender Inequality,' in Martha Nussbaum and Jonathan Glover, eds., *Women, Culture and Development: A Study of Human Capabilities*, Oxford: Clarendon Press.

Shapiro, Ian (1986), *The Evolution of Rights in Liberal Theory*, Cambridge: Cambridge University Press.

Shue, Henry (1980), *Basic Rights*, Princeton, NJ: Princeton University Press.

Simon, L. Julian (1981), *The Ultimate Resource*, Princeton, NJ: Princeton University Press.

Singer, Peter (1996), 'Famine, Affluence, and Morality,' in William Aiken and Hugh LaFollette (eds), *World Hunger and Morality*, 2nd edn, Upper Saddle River, NJ: Prentice Hall.

Skidelsky, Robert (1983), *John Maynard Keynes: Hopes Betrayed 1883–1920*, New York: Penguin Books.

Skidelsky, Robert (1992), *John Maynard Keynes: The Economist as Savior 1920–1937*, New York: Penguin Books.

Slade, David C. Esq. (ed.) (1990), *Putting the Public Trust Doctrine to Work*, Obtained from the Coastal States Association.

Smart, J. J. C. and Williams, Bernard (1973), *Utilitarianism For and Against*, Cambridge: Cambridge University Press.

Spencer, Herbert (1969), *Social Statics: or, The Conditions Essential to Human Happiness Specified, and the First of them Developed*, New York: A. M. Kelley.

Stamp Dawkins, Marian (1985), 'The Scientific Basis for Assessing Suffering in Animals,' in Peter Singer (ed.), *In Defence of Animals*, Oxford: Blackwell Publishers.

Stegner, Wallace (1991), *A Sense of Place*, New York: Viking Penguin.

Stokey, Edith and Zeckhauser, Richard (1978), *A Primer for Policy Analysis,* New York: W. W. Norton Co.

Susskind, Lawrence E. (1994), *Environmental Diplomacy: Negotiating More Effective Global Agreements*, Oxford: Oxford University Press.

Tawney, R. H. (1959), *The Idea of Equality*, quoted from George L. Abernathy (ed.), *The Idea of Equality*, Richmond, VA: John Knox Press.

Taylor, Paul W. (1986), *Respect for Nature: A Theory of Environmental Ethics*, Princeton: Princeton University Press.

Thomas, Keith (1983), *Man and the Natural World: A History of the Modern Sensibility*, New York: Pantheon Books.

Thoreau, Henry David (1967) [1849], *Walden and Resistance to Civil Government*, New York: Twayne Publishers.

Trevelyan, George Macaulay (1953), *History of England*, Garden City, NY: Doubleday.

Tuchman, Barbara W. (1978), *A Distant Mirror: The Calamitous 14th Century*, New York: Knopf.

Turner, Frederick Jackson (1921), *The Frontier in American History*, New York: Henry Holt and Company.

Turner, R. Kerry (ed.) (1993), *Sustainable Environmental Economics and Management: Principles and Practice*, London: Belhaven Press.

Vogel, Joseph Henry (1994), *Genes for Sale: Privatization as a Conservation Policy*, New York: Oxford University Press.

Walzer, Michael (1983), *Spheres of Justice: A Defense of Pluralism*, New York: Basic Books.

Wapner, Paul (1997), *Global Governance*, Cambridge, MA: MIT Press.

Wargo, John (1996), *Our Children's Toxic Legacy: How Science and Law Fail to Protect Us from Pesticides*, New Haven, CT: Yale University Press.

Wasserman, David (1998), 'Consumption, Appropriation and Stewardship,' in David A. Crocker and Toby Linden (eds), *The Ethics of Consumption: The Good Life, Justice, and Global Stewardship*, Lanham, MD: Rowman and Littlefield Publishers.

Weber, Max (1958), *The City*, Glencoe, IL: The Free Press.

Weiner, Jonathan (1995), *The Beak of the Finch*, New York: Vintage Books.

Weiss, Edith Brown (1984), 'The Planetary Trust: Conservation and Intergenerational Equity,' *Ecology Law Quarterly*, vol. II, no. 4, pp. 495–581.

Weiss, Edith Brown (1988), *In Fairness to Future Generations: International Law, Common Patrimony, and Intergenerational Equity*, Tokyo: The United Nations University.

White, Lynn (1967), 'Historical Roots of our Ecological Crisis,' *Science*, 10 March, pp. 1203–7.

World Bank (1992), *World Development Report 1992*, Oxford: Oxford University Press.

World Commission on Environment and Development (1987), *Our Common Future*, New York: Oxford University Press.

World Resources Institute (1990), *World Resources*, New York: Oxford University Press.

World Resources Institute (1998), *1998–99 World Resources: Environmental Change and Human Health*, New York: Oxford University Press.

Worster, Donald (1990), 'The Ecology of Order and Chaos,' *Environmental History and Review*, Summer/Spring, pp. 1–18.

Wrangham, Richard and Peterson, Dale (1996), *Demonic Males*, Boston, MA: Houghton Mifflin.

Yergin, Daniel (1977), *Shattered Peace: The Origins of the Cold War and the National Security State*, Boston, MA: Houghton Mifflin Co.

Young, Iris (1990), *Justice and the Politics of Difference*, Princeton: Princeton University Press.

Zaelke, Durwood, Orbuch, Paul and Housman, Robert F. (eds) (1993), *Trade and the Environment: Law, Economics and Policy*, Washington, DC: Island Press.

Zajac, Edward E. (1985), 'Perceived Economic Justice: The Example of Public Utility Regulation,' in H. Peyton Young (ed.), *Cost Allocation: Methods, Principles, Applications*, Elsevier Science Publishers, pp. 119–53.

Zimmerman, Michael E. (1990), 'Deep Ecology and Ecofeminism: The Emerging Debate,' in Irene Diamond and Gloria Feman Orenstein (eds), *Reweaving the World: The Emergence of Ecofeminism*, San Francisco: Sierra Club Books.

APPENDIX:
INDICES OF GLOBAL
ENVIRONMENTAL DISRUPTIONS
DUE TO HUMAN ACTIVITIES

Index	Natural Baseline	Anthropogenic Disruption due to				Human Natural
		Agriculture	Traditional Energy Supply	Industrial Energy Supply	Other Activities	
Land Use (km^2)	135,000,000 total ice-free land	15,000,000 cultivated (⅔ harvested)	5,000,000 to sustain fuel-wood supply	150,000 (⅔ hydro)	1,500,000 cities, transportation	0.15
Water Use (km^3/yr)	50,000 total runoff (⅔ unusable)	2,000 irrigation	?	800 process, cooling, evaporation	500 all other	0.2 (of usable)
CO_2 Emissions (Gt C/yr)	150 net primary productivity	0–1 forest clearing	0.2 deforestation for fuelwood	6.3 fossil-fuel combustion	0–0.5 lumber, cement urbanization	0.004/yr
CO_2 Added (Gt C)	594 preindustrial atmosphere	100	40	260	10	0.31
CH_4 Emissions (Mt C)	160 wetlands, termites, ocean	210 ruminants, paddies, burning	?	100 natural gas, coal mines	65 landfills, sewage	2.3
Nitrogen Fixation (Mt N/yr)	200 biological fixation	60 fertilizer	1	30 fossil-fuel combustion	1 industrial processes	0.5
N_2O Emissions (Mt N/yr)	9 oceans, soil	4.4 soils, burning ruminants	?	?	1.3 industrial processes	0.4

Index	Natural Baseline	Anthropogenic Disruption due to				Human Natural
		Agriculture	Traditional Energy Supply	Industrial Energy Supply	Other Activities	
Sulfur Emissions (Mt S/yr)	100 decay, sea spray	0.8 burning	0.3 burning	60 coal, oil burning	10 smelting	0.7
React. HC Emissions (Mt/yr)	800 vegetation	30 burning	4 burning	30 combustion, refining	20 industrial processes	0.1
Particulate Emissions (Mt/yr)	500 sea spray, volcanoes, dust	40 burning wheat handling	15 burning	40 fossil-fuel combustion	50 industrial processes	0.3
Lead Emissions (kt Pb/yr)	25 volcanoes, dust	0.4 burning	0.2 burning	230 gasoline additives	100 metals production	13
Mercury Emissions (kt Hg/yr)	25 outgassing	0.7 burning, biocides	0.2 burning	3 oil, coal burning	13 mining, mobilization	0.7
Oil Added to Oceans (Mt/yr)	0.5 natural seeps	—	—	3 tankers, platforms	2 lube-oil disposal, waste	10
Radiation (million person-rem)	800 radon, cosmic rays	?	—	1 reactors, coal burning	150 medical, fallout	0.2

INDEX

PLANET EARTH

The Latest Weapon of War
Rosalie Bertell

As weaponry and warfare have become more sophisticated, so their long-term effects have become more insidious and deadly. Whilst it is easy to identify the visible aftermath of war, how can we gauge less obvious costs such as poverty, famine, environmental problems and civil unrest? Each year governments pump huge amounts of money into military research programs but what do we really know about the long-term consequences?

In *Planet Earth*, Rosalie Bertell proposes that the key to understanding the impact of future wars lies in a close analysis of the past. She shows how the quest for military power has destabilized the delicate natural balance of the earth's ecosystem, causing widespread devastation in environmental, economic and social terms and calls for a new approach to security, which rises above national agendas to seek global solutions to a global problem.

> Planet Earth deserves a wide audience. Rosalie Bertell's ground-breaking work *No Immediate Danger* sounded the alarm on the understated problems associated with the nuclear fuel cycle. With *Planet Earth*, she has again unearthed a wealth of disturbing, almost unbelievable information. A no-nonsense writer who presents stark facts in an accessible fashion, Bertell builds her compelling case with care and solid methodology.
> —Matthew Behrens, Quill & Quire

Scientist DR ROSALIE BERTELL is a respected activist and lecturer, founder of several organizations, including the International Institute of Concern for Public Health, in Toronto, and the recipient of numerous awards and honorary doctorates. Dr Bertell is a member of a Roman Catholic religious congregation, the Grey Nuns of the Sacred Heart.

272 pages
Paperback ISBN: 1-55164-182-8 $24.99
Hardcover ISBN: 1-55164-183-6 $53.99

MAKING WAVES

The Origins and Future of

Greenpeace

Jim Bohlen

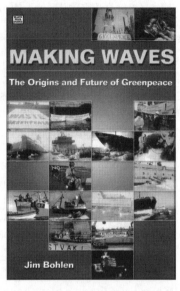

In 1971, when nuclear tests were being carried out on a small island off the coast of Alaska, a small group of people, believing that a few individuals could make a difference, set sail on an old fishing boat determined to put an end to the testing.

Few dreamed they would go on to become the largest environmental protection agency in the world. Today, with offices in over thirty countries, supported by more than three million members worldwide, accredited with more than twenty-six international treaties, Greenpeace remains an independent, non-partisan and non-profit organization.

Written as a memoir by one of the founders, this book is an important part of the history of the environmental movement. It is about the origins of the organization; about the identity and motivation of the people first involved, their adventures and experiences; and about the development of the high profile direct action campaign methods which work for Greenpeace even to this day.

Originally a research scientist, JIM BOHLEN helped to found the Sierra Club in Canada, and later the breakaway organization that would come to be known as Greenpeace. In 1974, Jim and his wife Marie established a homestead on an island north of Vancouver, where they experimented in the development of an energy and food self-reliant lifestyle. In 1983 Jim was involved with the founding of the Green Party of Canada and stood for election to Parliament in 1984 and 1988. Jim served as a director of Greenpeace Canada until 1993, when he retired to his island paradise to write and help with policy development for the Green Party.

224 pages, photographs
Paperback ISBN: 1-55164-166-6 $19.99
Hardcover ISBN: 1-55164-167-4 $48.99

MURRAY BOOKCHIN READER

Janet Biehl, editor

This collection provides an overview of the thought of the foremost social theorist and political philosopher of the libertarian left today. His writings span five decades, and subject matter of remarkable breadth.

Bookchin's writings on revolutionary philosophy, politics, and history are far less known than the specific controversies that have surrounded him, but they are deserving of far greater attention.

Consistent throughout his work is a search for ways to replace today's capitalist society with a more rational and humane alternative.

A major American political philosopher.
—San Francisco Chronicle

His books are classic statements of contemporary anarchism.
—The Independent

Murray Bookchin stands at the pinnacle of the genre of utopian social criticism.   —The Village Voice

Murray Bookchin's books are of critical importance.
—New Scientist

JANET BIEHL is also the author of *Finding Our Way: Rethinking Ecofeminist Politics*, and, with Murray Bookchin, *Politics of Social Ecology*, both published by Black Rose Books. She lectures at the Institute of Social Ecology in Plainfield, Vermont. MURRAY BOOKCHIN, Professor Emeritus at the School of Environmental Studies, Ramapo College and Director Emeritus of the Institute of Social Ecology, has authored more than a dozen books on urbanism, ecology, technology and philosophy. For those interested in exploring more deeply his ideas, Black Rose Books has published nine of these titles.

288 pages, bibliography, index
Paperback ISBN: 1-55164-118-6 $24.99
Hardcover ISBN: 1-55164-119-4 $53.99